Country Roads
~ of ~
NEW HAMPSHIRE

A Guide Book
from Country Roads Press

SECOND EDITION

Country Roads
~ of ~
NEW HAMPSHIRE

Steve Sherman

Illustrated by
Dawn L. Nelson

Country Roads Press
CASTINE • MAINE

Country Roads of New Hampshire
© 1993 by Steve Sherman. All rights reserved.

Second edition, 1995.

Published by Country Roads Press
P.O. Box 286, Lower Main Street
Castine, Maine 04421

Text and cover design by Edith Allard, Coopers Mills, Maine.
Cover illustration by Victoria Sheridan.
Typesetting by Camden Type 'n Graphics.

ISBN 1-56626-095-7

Library of Congress Cataloging-in-Publication Data
Sherman, Steve
     Country roads of New Hampshire / Steve Sherman ;
  illustrated by Dawn L. Nelson. — 2nd ed.
          p.   cm.
     Includes index.
     ISBN 1-56626-095-7 : $9.95
       1. New Hampshire—Tours.   2. Automobile travel—
  New Hampshire—Guidebooks.   I. Title.
  F32.3.S48   1995
  917.4204'43—dc20   94-45632
                                                      CIP

Printed in the United States of America.
10 9 8 7 6 5 4 3 2 1

My body is dancing to the songs of the country,
the church bell that rings every Sunday at nine,
to baseball and bike riding through the middle of town
past the one-family store with the awnings pulled down.

—from "Quadrilling Through Thyme"
by Julia Older

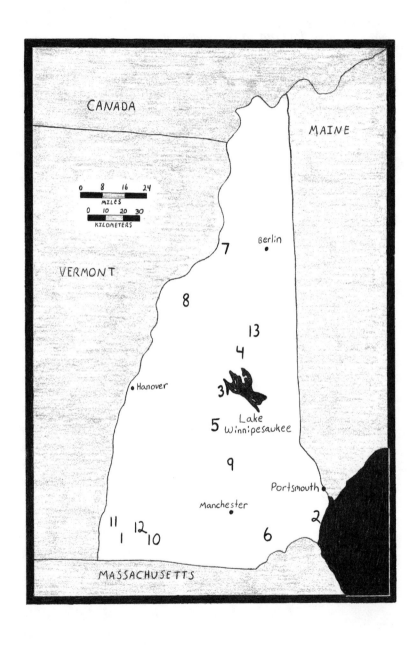

Contents

(& Key to New Hampshire Country Roads)

Introduction

The classic story about road travel tells of a local who answers a lost stranger's question with, "Nope, you can't get there from here." Variations include, "Well, are you Republican or Democrat?" and "Depends on where you're from." Touring back roads challenges the impossible, like the man who stopped his horse and hayload at the entrance to a covered bridge, studied the scene, turned and left. He figured he could get into the bridge all right, but just couldn't squeeze through the hole at the other end. Perspective is all—the reason that some lovers of New England say, "Why travel when I'm already here?"

Why travel through New Hampshire? There are lots of reasons, the first being that this extraordinary state offers endless stories to discover and histories to study. Rural New Hampshire also contains a sumptuous number of lakes, rivers, mountains, marshes—and the White Mountain Range with the highest peak in the Northeast; Lake Winnipesaukee, among the largest in-state lakes in the nation; Grand Monadnock with a six-state view; the craggy seacoast's tidal inlets; and the gorgeous gorges of Franconia and Crawford notches. The list goes on and on: pristine ponds, inscrutable swamps, wildlife wilderness.

Human-scale towns and villages match this bounty of geography. Nearly everywhere you drive there are deep-rooted villages comfortingly surrounded by nature. Fresh air and water. Handsome woods and boulder-strewn brooks. Proud, clean highways and byways.

All this presents itself in six regions of the Granite State: the Seacoast, Merrimack Valley, Monadnock, Dartmouth/ Lake Sunapee, Lakes, and White Mountain regions. The trips described in this book cover all six regions from the arrowhead point of the state to the broad southern base. Trips follow part of the Connecticut River western border of New Hampshire as well as the eastern seacoast, plus both flashy and subdued attractions in between.

Fortunately, New Hampshire is an accessible size; none of these trips requires a frantic, overnight rush to reach. And along the way you'll pass some of the 40,000 miles of streams, 2,000 lakes and ponds, and 182 mountains over 3,000 feet elevation (with 1,300 trail miles in the White Mountains alone).

Statistics can be impressive—the fastest wind speed in the world recorded at the summit of Mt. Washington, for example, was 231 mph in 1934. But more impressive are the seasons—the exuberant confetti of autumn leaves, the meringue-colored mountains of snowy winter, the maple-sugar harvest of early spring, the robust swagger of summer. No ho-hum blandness here.

Country Roads of New Hampshire speaks for and about country roads, not city streets. Designed for giving ideas of where to go and what to know, the book is also meant to be read and enjoyed in itself. Please use it as both a guide and a companion.

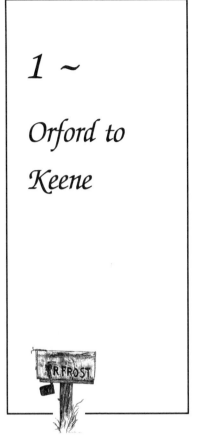

1 ~
Orford to
Keene

From Concord: Take I-89 north to White River Junction, Vermont, then I-91 north to exit 15 at Fairlee, Vermont. Drive across the Connecticut River to Orford, New Hampshire, and Route 10 south. This trip runs approximately 81 miles.

Highlights: *The Connecticut River Valley, easy rolling hills, cornfields, Ridge Row, St. Gaudens National Historical Site, the longest wooden covered bridge in the U.S., roadside stands, Dartmouth College.*

Orford and Ridge Row

Set far back from Route 10, which doubles as Main Street, several stately white mansions overlook otherwise unpretentious Orford. The Ridge Row houses were built between 1773 and 1839 and conjure up images of prosperous gentlefolk driving horses and buggies up their quarter-mile entrances. White fences, hefty maples and oaks, and long spreads of well-kept lawns complete the country elegance. Originally, the houses were built for professionals and businessmen. The John Wheeler House, constructed in 1814–16, the southern

1

most in the row, was designed by Asher Benjamin, a Boston architect and associate of Charles Bulfinch, the famous American designer of cathedrals and institutional buildings.

Across the street lies an abruptly different scene—Weeks' General Store, established 1804. You can still find apple cider and cheddar cheese wheels here. Like most general stores, this one also serves as the town's news-and-views shop.

Next door, the Orford Social Library, with its white picket fence and geraniums, stands guard for democracy. The New Hampshire small-town library acts as the moral equivalent of flint and musket. Big or minuscule, public libraries mean public access to information, the bedrock of the Republic. This reassuring heritage continues wherever you travel in the Granite State. In fact, these libraries can be lodestars of a region and often include historical rooms that feature old photographs, maps, and books worth exploring.

When you head south out of town on Main Street/Route 10, you're quickly into cornfields and fallow fields. You'll see some Pennsylvania Dutch-style barns half-set into the earth for easy loading of hay and gangly harvesting machinery. A white horse or two might be lazing in the fields.

Lyme

After about three and a half miles, the Lyme town line marker appears on the right-hand side of the road. Another three and a half miles through this slow-motion country, and you come to Post Pond, a town recreation area. Park your car and stretch your legs. If by chance you're toting a canoe, the pond has good access and is a congenial place for paddling through lily pads.

A very short distance from the public access, look for Loch Lyme Lodge, a 125-acre lakeside complex of cottages. After more than seventy years, the lodge is still rustic—"No telephones, no televisions, simple furnishings, no credit cards accepted, no wall-to-wall carpeting, no video arcade, no hot tubs, no microwaves, and no bar with nightly entertainment." Instead, you'll find fresh air, clean water, stars in the clear night sky, and a Sunday night lakeside buffet. Now that's country vacationing.

As you move on down Route 10, you'll soon come to the Lyme green, a long, narrow strip of repose at the town center. The spire of the Lyme Congregational Church rises up at one end of the green. Behind the white church stand twenty-seven red horse-and-carriage stalls, which in the old days were assigned to families who attended Sunday service. You'll want to take a photo of this, it has that beckoning appeal. It's a good bet that a local will come along and say, "Taking pictures of them is about all they're good for now."

*A typical New England country store, on the common
in Lyme, New Hampshire*

The Lyme Inn, right across the way at the end of the village green, was built in 1809. The popular way station retains a rural yet updated ambiance. Furnishings differentiate each room, and ten fireplaces add a final, comforting touch.

Be sure to stop at the Lyme Country Store on the Route 10 side of the common. Bright and clean, the store fits the concept of early sheep-raising Lyme, chartered in 1761 and named after Lyme Regis in England.

About two miles down Route 10 from the center of Lyme, you'll notice a complex of about a dozen freestanding, refurbished old buildings on the right. This is an office park, but if you happen to arrive at dinnertime and favor French cuisine, head for D'Artagnan, located downstairs in the building facing the entrance driveway.

Otherwise, continue cruising Route 10 south. The road opens up a little more in this next stretch of about six miles, paralleling the Connecticut River for extended views. The highway shoulder widens here, and you'll probably see bicyclists along this section. When you pass the Cold Regions Research & Engineering Laboratory on the right (where some of the world's most exotic research on ice and polar conditions are studied), you'll know you're approaching Hanover.

Hanover and Lebanon

Winter or summer, autumn or spring, Dartmouth College and Hanover fulfill the storybook picture of a classic Ivy League campus and town. Follow the Route 10 signs around a long block to take you through the center of Hanover. You'll pass the red-brick Hanover Inn, with its graceful arches and white-pillared porch directly opposite the expansive Dartmouth College green. Studious-looking Dartmouth Hall from the late 1700s overlooks the green to the right, while the Baker Library tower chimes the hours at the far end of the quad.

In February, you can stroll among the ice sculptures of the Winter Carnival. In the fall, you can rustle through the leaves on the quad. And in the spring and summer, you can join students soaking up the sunshine. Everywhere you look, fountain-like elms and sturdy maples add deep roots to this tradition-minded college.

As you might expect, you'll see a lot if you're inclined to get off the road and stay awhile in this collegial town of 9,000. Next to the Hanover Inn is the Hood Museum of Art. The Hopkins Center for the Performing Arts stages plays and concerts in summer and winter. Near the Baker Library is the Stefansson Collection of prized Arctic and Eskimo artifacts. And, of course, if you like to browse through books, the Dartmouth Coop on Main Street (Route 10) seems endless.

Steer straight down Main Street to drive out of Hanover on Route 10 south. In little more than two miles, the Connecticut River suddenly appears on the right, where the Wilder Hydroelectric Plant of the New England Power Company generates electricity. On the left, parking and picnic tables give you a rest and a big view of the complex. If you wish, you can take a short, pleasant hike along the Pine Grove Rim Trail beginning up the shady slope.

Another mile south, you'll pass through the outskirts of Lebanon. For the next 1.2 miles, you'll see signs for I-89. At a Y junction, notice the signs for Routes 4 and 10 pointing uphill to the left. Turn *right* at this junction and continue through the cramped Lebanon outskirts for about one mile until you see the I-89 overpass. Go straight under the overpass. Immediately on the right is a sign for St. Gaudens National Historical Site. Now on Route 12A, you'll see a confirming sign for this route as you pass several fast-food restaurants. Proceed up the hill and into the trees, and you'll be back on a nice country road.

Plainfield and the Cornish Colony

For about three miles after I-89 on Route 12A, the road narrows a bit and winds softly past cornfields and weathered barns, woods, and river views where the Connecticut keeps rolling along beside you.

Suddenly you'll come upon the Edgewater Farm. If you're at all inclined to buy produce, stop here. Besides, it's impossible to resist the parking lot rimmed with a fireworks of flowers—purples, reds, yellows, blues. The neat-and-trim farm stand was obviously built with the same hands and heart as the neat rows of broccoli, cabbage, lettuce, and other plants were sown. This is only part of the farm; the rest lies a short drive away on a side road along the river.

This is the kind of farm stand where the operators ask, "Would you like me to take the tops off these carrots for you?" You might end up taking home Edgewater Farm beets, tomatoes, peppers, and green beans.

Back in the car, head on down the road a couple of miles until you spot a small swamp on the right. A little farther along, a larger swamp appears on the left. Something about the word *swamp* chills the bones. But no murky monsters lurk here. This is just an intriguing part of nature with dead, bony trees protruding from the flat, dark water and lush grass.

In less than a mile, you'll emerge on a hilltop with a spectacular, sweeping view. These are the surprises and twists of scenery worth driving for. Chunky Mount Ascutney in Vermont dominates the far horizon.

The road and you slide down into the long valley, and in another mile you'll be easing through the center of Plainfield, built in 1761. The general store goes back to 1858, although "Videos and Fresh Grinders Made to Order" share the billing. Notice the old red-brick "Blow-Me-Down-Grange"; take out your camera for the sign if not for the building. Looking at this slumping building and others of the ilk reminds you how widely the Grange movement permeated the country at the turn of the century, when farming occupied most of the population and Granges were *the* agricultural and social meeting places.

A little more than one and a half miles beyond town, you'll see a small sign for Covered Bridge No. 23. A tree-lined dirt road leads a tenth of a mile or so to a small bridge. It gives you some perspective when, farther on down the main road, you pass the longest wooden covered bridge in the United States.

The next four miles or so take you into "literary country." The first sign of it is an historic marker about Winston Churchill (1871–1947)—not *the* Winston Churchill, but the best-selling American novelist. This Winston Churchill was the author of *Coniston* and other books. He called his nearby house Harlakenden House. It burned in 1923, but not before President Woodrow Wilson used it as a summer residence three times beginning in 1913.

Down the road a piece, you can't miss the historic marker at Blow-Me-Down Mill. This represents the Cornish Colony, which flourished here in the early part of this century. Writers and artists of all persuasions lived, worked, and played here. Over the years, the interacting groups became well-known for their contributions. Here's what the marker says:

The Cornish Colony (1883–1935) was a group of artists, sculptors, writers, journalists, poets, and musicians who joined the sculptor Augustus Saint Gaudens in Cornish and found the area a delightful place to live and work. Some prominent members were sculptor Herbert Adams, poet Percy MacKaye, architect Charles A. Platt, artists Kenyon Cox, Stephen Parrish and his son Maxfield, and landscape architects Rose Nichols and Ellen Shipman.

St. Gaudens National Historical Site

One-quarter mile after the Cornish Colony marker, turn left and follow the entrance road uphill to the St. Gaudens National Historical Site. You're in for a treat. At age thirty-seven, Augustus St. Gaudens (1848–1907), the renowned American sculptor, just couldn't take another city summer in New York. He ended up buying this hilltop house, transformed it into an enchanting home and studio of the American belle époque, and lived the last part of his life here.

A prickly description of the original house reads as follows: "an upright New England farmer with a new set of false teeth" and "like some austere and recalcitrant New England old maid struggling in the arms of a Greek Faun." But St. Gaudens fashioned the house into what you see now, which has been well preserved by the National Park Service.

You'll enjoy the tour through the house, the studio and exhibition room, and the classically attired grounds, with pillars, hedges, and quiet scenes graced with reproductions of his sculptures. Be sure to see *Adams Memorial* (of Henry Adams's wife), and *Diana* from Stanford White's tower on Madison Square Garden in New York City. St. Gaudens redesigned the $10 and $20 gold pieces (on display) and sculpted *Standing Lincoln*, the *Shaw Memorial* for the Boston Common, and many other well-recognized pieces. The museum is open from May to October.

Cornish-Windsor Bridge and Charlestown

Three miles down Route 12A south, which skirts the Connecticut River, you'll see a covered bridge with a sign overhead: "Walk your horse or pay a two dollar fine." But you're free from fines for driving your car through the bridge, which takes you across the river to Vermont. This ranks as one of the most photographed bridges (at least wooden bridges) in the world.

It measures 460 feet long and claims to be the longest two-span covered bridge in the world. In 1866, it cost $9,000 to build. You can scarcely buy one of the cars that goes across it for that now.

The bridge you see is the fourth one built over the years. Originally operated by a private corporation as a toll bridge, it was finally purchased by the state of New Hampshire in 1936. Not a state to raise taxes, New Hampshire kept charging the toll, at least until 1943.

Three-quarters of a mile farther on, Trinity Church will catch your eye on the left as you drive up a short, steep curve. The stark beauty of this strikingly plain, bare-bones church typifies some of the no-nonsense heritage of this countryside.

From here on, the road eases through about five miles of farm country, with Ascutney View Farms on the right. If you're itching to get back into city congestion, drive into Claremont and take a look at the rejuvenated Opera House in the main square. If you'd rather avoid city traffic, stay on Route 12A. Do this by crossing the Sugar River; the Route 12A sign is straight ahead.

Continue over the hills for about two miles, past some clean-technology factories. Stay straight on Route 12A (avoid the bypass to Routes 112 and 12). At a stop sign, turn right, and in a tenth of a mile, turn right onto Route 12 south (which is also Route 11 west). This wider road leads three and a half miles to Charlestown, with its broad Main Street, expansive lawns, and solid old houses.

Cruise on past town for three miles as the Connecticut River comes into sight again, flowing beside rich farmland. Drive right along the river for a couple of harmonious miles until you enter North Walpole, where the road cramps up. Stay on Route 12 as it doglegs around the river and the old power dam.

Walpole to Keene

Six miles south on Route 12 lies Walpole. Follow the second "Business District" sign. This takes you more directly to the older section of Walpole. Steer uphill to a stop sign, turn left, and mosey on down Main Street past the Unitarian Church (1761) and the white Victorian houses. This is a hillside town with a charming inn and newer sections farther on down Main Street as it winds through town.

Back on Route 12, you'll find the rest of the fifteen miles or so to Keene a pleasant drive. Stop at the Major Leonard Keep Restaurant on the right in East Westmoreland (accent the first syllable, and they'll figure you for a native) for a good country meal. If you'd rather move on, be sure to stop, about seven miles farther on, at the Summit Gift Barn on the right. Open and inviting, it has a large parking lot. Inside, Katherine Aldrich and her accommodating crew stock a wide array of gifts and goods.

You'll know you're heading into Keene when, about one and a half miles later, you drive down the other side of the summit and Grand Monadnock points skyward through the trees that line the end of this route.

In the Area

All phone numbers are within area code 603.

Baker Library, Dartmouth College, Hanover: 646-2560

D'Artagnan, Lyme: 795-2137

Dartmouth Coop, Hanover: 643-3616

Edgewater Farm, Lebanon: 298-5764

Hanover Inn: 643-4300

Hopkins Center for the Performing Arts, Dartmouth
    College, Hanover: 646-2422

Loch Lyme Lodge, Lyme: 795-2141

Lyme Inn: 795-2222 or 795-4404

Major Leonard Keep Restaurant, East Westmoreland: 399-4474

St. Gaudens National Historical Site, Cornish: 675-2175

Summit Gift Barn, East Westmoreland: 352-3321

2 ~

Hampton Beach to Portsmouth

From Boston: Take I-95 north to the New Hampshire border and exit 60, go east on New Hampshire Route 286, then to Route 1A north to Hampton Beach State Park. From Manchester take Route 101 east to Route 51 east, then to Route 1A south to Hampton Beach State Park. This trip runs approximately 25 miles.

Highlights: *Sand dunes and wide beaches of Hampton Beach State Park, Rye Harbor and Marina, Isles of Shoals, Odiorne Point State Park, Seacoast Science Center, lighthouses, lobstermen, Runnymede horse farm, Fuller Gardens, Fort Constitution, seventeenth-century homes.*

The Hamptons

To travel north on Route 1A, begin at the north side of the bridge to Seabrook Beach. At this point, you'll see the Hampton Harbor State Marina and Harbor, where deep-sea fishing boats advertise their trips. Straight across the inlet stands the Seabrook Nuclear Power Station, its giant domes protruding from the low horizon of tree and sea. Expose yourself to the glories of nuclear power; an exhibit hall awaits you on US 1.

If you want to begin this seacoast trip with wonderful sand and sea, drive into the new Hampton Beach State Park opposite the Marina and Harbor. You won't be able to see the beach and waves from your car, so take the time to follow the paths over the dunes. These low-lying, natural seawall dunes, covered with grasses that trap the blowing sand, protect the land behind them during extraordinarily high tides and flooding storms.

At the crest of the dunes, an expanse of clean, white, rock-free beach delights the eye. The beach slants languorously to the shoreline, where white-green waves crash and splash from the horizon.

Remember this aesthetic feast when you return to Route 1A north, especially if it's summer. Now you're going to car-crawl through a dense human forest of summertime congestion. Metered parking blocks you from the North Beach of Hampton, where arcades, motels, slush stands, and T-shirt booths draw a crowd. Be patient, enjoy the display of human possibilities, and know that better traveling lies ahead.

After about one mile of this, you'll see signs for Route 51 and to I-95. The congestion thins, and the Atlantic is more often visible on the other side of the beach wall. Go through the traffic signal at Route 27. In a couple of miles, you'll be moving into a more typical New Hampshire coastline area, with salt marshes inland on the left and properly weathered beach houses on the right. A little more than two and a half miles from Route 17, Route 1A passes beautiful North Hampton State Beach, then curves around an outcrop of ancient sea boulders. At the top of the hill, Route 111 awaits you.

Horses and Roses

For a short side trip, turn left onto Route 111 west at an ocean overlook. Slightly less than one mile down the road, you'll drive through an open expanse of fenced fields and big barns with grain silos—the Runnymede Farm of Rye. If you drive to the main field bordered by a stone wall and roses, you may see the horses. A giant sign with photographs commemorates the farm's two champions: "Mom's Command," Champion, 1985 N.Y. Filly Triple Crown; and "Dancer's Image," Winner, 1968 Kentucky Derby.

Backtrack on Route 111 to Route 1A. As you ascend the slight grade, a sea gull's view of North Hampton State Beach appears on your right. Turn left onto Route 1A at the stop sign and enjoy the seemingly endless ocean ahead and its rocky edge below.

In one-tenth of a mile, a small green sign with yellow letters, hanging demurely on the left at the first block from Route 111, announces the Fuller Gardens. Turn into the narrow, shaded street, and in another tenth of a mile, the tan pebble parking lot for the gardens appears on the left.

When Massachusetts governor Alvan Fuller died in 1958, the Fuller Foundation of New Hampshire assumed maintenance of the governor's summer estate and gardens. Stroll through the array of 1,500 rose bushes and other flowers, hedges, award-winning annuals, greenhouses, and lush lawns. Don't forget to visit the Japanese garden.

Rye

Turn left from the Fuller Gardens on the one-way street, and reach Route 1A one-half mile later. If you'd like to see some grand oceanside mansions, turn right and drive along the part of Route 1A that you bypassed for the gardens. The road wanders past stretches of lawn and driveways in front of flashy or sophisticated (depending on your outlook) seaside homes from another era.

This section of Route 1A north winds along the shoreline, which is sometimes in sight over the seawall. One mile from the Fuller Gardens, follow the S curve around a private beach club. Cruise past smallish Jenness State Park and onward through small village centers.

A scene along New Hampshire's working coastline

Along much of this section, salt marshes line the road on the left. Animals and vegetables feed on the powerful nutrients of these tidewater inlets. Yellow-centered white lilies and their green pads bloom in deep summer across huge expanses of these marshes. When the inlets drain, long-legged snowy egrets and small blue herons browse in the muck.

About a mile and a quarter past Jenness State Park, you'll pass a marker at the site of the Atlantic cable station. The receiving station for the first Atlantic telegraph cable was built here in 1874.

The surrounding prehistoric sunken forest is fascinating. Great cedar trees thrived here 3,200 years ago. Now stump remnants eight to ten feet in circumference are buried under twelve to fifteen feet of water and sand. They've been uncovered only two times in relatively recent history: at extremely low tide after severe storms in August 1889 and April 1958.

A tenth of a mile farther along you'll see the Pilot House Restaurant on the right next to a long blanket of marsh grass.

Soon after, a big sign marks the Saunders at Rye Harbor Restaurant. Turn right onto the access road to Saunders (with a wonderful patio overlooking the harbor) but continue past the restaurant for three-tenths of a mile. Not many people take this little detour because it looks like a squeezy road to nowhere. But it leads to the tip of the Rye Harbor breakwater, with lucky houses on the side. Pull into the turnaround, shut off the engine, and enjoy the Atlantic for a while.

Return to Route 1A, go another very short distance, and you'll pass the entrance to Rye Harbor and Marina. At this small working harbor, bait and tackle shops sell their wares. Whale-watching trips and sightseeing excursions to the Isles of Shoals take off here, too.

About a half mile farther around a sharp curve, you'll come to Rye Harbor State Park and Ragged Neck picnic area on the right of another sharp curve. A short, narrow jut of land invites you to take a lingering look and perhaps enjoy a meal out among the sea gulls and sailboats.

Two miles north, with more calm salt marshes on the left, you'll find Wallis Sands State Beach, a favorite swimming spot for many families. The appealing beach measures 150 feet wide at high tide and is 800 feet long. On the left, rocky coves with tidal pools attract youngsters, while on the right, a breakwater keeps the swimming enjoyable.

After curving around this beach, you'll go up a slight incline to a delightful overlook. One-half mile farther along is another overlook. You may be prompted to ask, "What *are* those islands out there?"

The Isles of Shoals

Six miles out to sea, the cliffs, scrub brush, and sugar-white buildings shimmering on the horizon draw your eye to the history-laden Isles of Shoals. Captain John Smith first sailed around them in 1614, and in the years to follow they grew in stature and importance as colonial British outposts and later American literary gathering spots. New Hampshire claims four of the islands, Maine five.

Through the centuries, so many noble and ignoble events have happened on the Isles that the history of the New Hampshire seacoast would be vastly different without them. Norwegian fishermen and their families developed the Isles into one of the world's great sources of the legendary dunfish (dried cod). The pirate Blackbeard buried treasure on the Isles, and ghosts at Babb's Cove are reported even today. (The wraith of a forsaken fisherman's wife is said to appear on the seaward rocks now and then.) An ax murder of two Norwegian women was an infamous crime of the nineteenth century.

Celia Thaxter, daughter of Thomas Laighton, who kept the whale-oil lighthouse at White Island and later built the 500-room Appledore Hotel, hosted the first true American literary and artistic salon in the late 1800s. Her friends and guests included John Greenleaf Whittier, Nathaniel Hawthorne, Ralph Waldo Emerson, Harriet Beecher Stowe, William Mason, and Childe Hassam.

Thaxter's poetry—written on Appledore Island—was widely published, her flower garden extravagantly admired, her books constantly reprinted. (*An Island Garden* became her most famous.) A novel by Julia Older, *The Island Queen*, captures the era when Thaxter reigned.

Today the Isles of Shoals remain as enchanting as in the past, but activities there have changed. Cornell University and the University of New Hampshire Marine Laboratory own and operate Appledore Island as a science research station. The Unitarian-Universalists own and conduct nondenominational summer workshops on Star Island. You can take a ferry from Portsmouth or Rye Harbor to the Isles of Shoals from spring through fall.

Odiorne

A little more than a mile along Route 1A you'll come to the 137-acre Odiorne Point State Park. Many picnic tables line the rocky shore, offering a wonderful view of the outlying entrance to Portsmouth harbor. Be sure to visit the new Seacoast Science Center, which features exhibits, area maps, and a gift shop.

Because of the lay of the land, this point attracted Native Americans during their summer migrations, but no one settled here until British immigrant David Thompson arrived in 1623. As fishing and fish processing developed, the growing commercial activities on the nearby shore became increasingly valuable, especially for the pirate Dixie Bull a decade later.

John Odiorne bought the land in 1660. From then until the Second World War, when the U.S. government took it over for defense purposes, the point remained in the Odiorne family. Cannon bunkers disguised as knolls were built to protect the navy yards. When two 16-inch guns were test-fired in 1944, the vibrations broke windows up and down the coast. The cannons were never fired again.

As a curious footnote, years later after the war, when a former German submarine captain was bringing in a freighter, he was asked whether he needed help in maneuvering into Portsmouth harbor. He replied, "Oh, no, during the war I went in many times."

New Castle

Two miles north of the Odiorne park entrance, you'll see Foyes Corner, which sells take-out food and groceries. Follow Route 1A to the right. One-half mile later, you'll see Route 1B to the right, with an adjacent sign for Wentworth-by-the-Sea.

Route 1B makes a longish curve through the old town of New Castle and approaches Portsmouth through much more pleasant oceanside country than if you continue on Route 1A.

In less than a mile, the Wentworth-by-the-Sea golf course opens up before you. Straight ahead, you'll see the majestic old hotel (if deconstructionists haven't demolished the cherished landmark, as promised), its regal Victorian splendor still visible in its turretlike towers and weathered elegance. Downhill a short distance, a right turn takes you to the Wentworth-by-the-Sea Marina, full of oceangoing yachts.

One-half mile farther along, the New Castle Public Library marks a right turn to the New Castle Common. This park follows the shore and invites you to spend some time looking at lighthouses, an old house on a wee island, bulging sails on sleek boats, and lobstermen everywhere.

Less than one-half mile up Route 1B is the U.S. Coast Guard station, beside Fort Constitution, a Revolutionary War outpost. At the turnoff to the fort, a marker across from the 1676 J. Morse House tells this tale:

> Dec. 14–15, 1774, several hundred men overpowered the small British garrison at Castle William & Mary, now Fort Constitution, New Castle, and removed quantities of military supplies. These raids, set off by Paul Revere's ride to Portsmouth on Dec. 13, were among the first overt acts of the American Revolution.

Don't miss the muscular Coast Guard ships to the left or the white lighthouse to the right behind the headquarters. Walk through the gate, as instructed, to the remains of Fort Constitution. This red-brick garrison commands a daunting edge of land at the entrance to Portsmouth harbor. No wonder the site held such strategic importance.

Return to Route 1B, and a tenth of a mile later, you'll pass through New Castle center. Turn right at the first block, where a sign for Ricker Lobster Co. points the way to an old neighborhood street. Turn left at the next block and cruise by the Portsmouth Yacht Club and the Piscataqua River. Along the way, you'll see homes dating to the seventeenth century. New Castle is situated on The Great Island, settled in 1623 and incorporated in 1693, one of the oldest New World hometowns.

After winding through a tight core of houses for less than one-half mile, turn right onto Route 1B. A mile later, you'll see the old graveyard on your left. A tidewater inlet invites you to slow down for classic seashore views on both sides of the road. Across the harbor on the right rise the huge cranes of the old navy shipyard.

Veer right at a Y junction. Follow the sign to Sanders Lobster Pound on Route 1B, then continue on toward Portsmouth.

Portsmouth

About one-half mile from the Y junction, drive up a house-crowded street with the Children's Museum (a converted church) on the left. Proceed downhill to another intriguing old settlement, Strawbery Banke.

The trip ends here, but Portsmouth is such a welcoming town that you should take a look around. Start with Strawbery Banke, a neighborhood museum that survived the urban renewal demolition crews of the 1950s. Thirty of the thirty-five historic houses from the seventeenth to twentieth centuries stand on their original foundations. All sorts of exhibits and demonstrations take you back in time on this 350-year-old site, once known as Puddle Dock.

A charming place anytime, Strawbery Banke especially delights visitors in December, when it's decorated for the holidays. In summer, Prescott Park, across the street along the harbor, blooms with an award-winning All-American flower garden. Irresistible.

Walk the downtown streets to get a feeling for the "olde tyme" in our time. Red-trimmed tugboats dock near Ceres

Street; Isles of Shoals cruises leave from Barker Wharf on Market Street. If you like good food, Portsmouth has an extravagant array of restaurants, some of them nationally known, others hidden tastefully along the back streets lined with centuries-old buildings.

In the Area

All phone numbers are within area code 603.

Atlantic Fishing Fleet, Rye Harbor: 964-5220

Children's Museum of Portsmouth: 436-3853

Fuller Gardens, North Hampton: 964-5414

Hampton Beach State Park: 926-3784

Isles of Shoals Steamship Co., Portsmouth: 431-5500 or 800-441-4620

Jenness State Beach, Rye: 436-6607

N.H. Seacoast Cruises, Rye Harbor: 964-5545 or 800-734-6488

North Hampton State Beach: 436-6607

Oceanic Whale Watch Expeditions, Portsmouth: 431-5500 or 800-441-4620

Portsmouth Harbor Cruises: 436-8084 or 800-776-0915

Saunders at Rye Harbor: 964-6466

Seacoast Science Center at Odiorne Point State Park, Rye: 436-8043

Strawbery Banke, Portsmouth: 433-1100

Wallis Sands State Beach, Rye: 436-9404

Wentworth-by-the-Sea, Rye: 433-5010

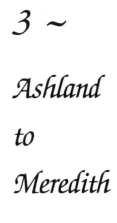

3 ~

Ashland

to

Meredith

From Concord: Take I-93 north to exit 24, then east on Route 3. The course nearly encircles Lake Winnipesaukee and returns to exit 23 on I-93. This trip runs approximately 82 miles.

Highlights: *Squam Lake, the Science Center, Castle in the Clouds, the Libby Museum, Wolfeboro, Weirs Beach, farm stands.*

Ashland to Center Harbor

From the beginning, water marks this trip. Leave I-93 at exit 24 and take US 3 toward the center of Ashland, a handy town to start this excursion into popular, and sometimes populous, terrain. In three-quarters of a mile, US 3 (to Holderness) turns left at an Ashland town park slanting to the Little Squam River. The river shows itself intermittently for a mile out of Ashland, birthplace and early home of George Hoyt Whipple, Nobel Prize winner in medicine in 1934 for his work on pernicious anemia.

A reassuring sight comes only a mile later at River Street, on the right. New Hampshireites are still constructing wooden covered bridges, and this one, number 65, is charming. You can see it from US 3, but take a few minutes to drive over it, with the river on the right and Little Squam Lake on the left. Built by Milton Graton in 1990, the bridge continues a long tradition in New Hampshire, which sports more covered bridges than any of the other five New England states.

No one knows for certain when the first wooden covered bridge was built in New Hampshire, but they were certainly constructed by the eighteenth century. The bridges were covered to protect the supporting trusses from the weather, not, as some may think, to keep snow from accumulating on them. (In fact, snow was shoveled onto bridges for sleigh travel.)

Bridge builder Milton Graton has his own long history of bridges. He's built and repaired covered bridges all his life. In his hometown of Ashland, he built a 140-foot covered bridge for Woodstock, Vermont, in 1968. After dismantling it and shipping it to Woodstock, he reassembled it and pulled it

Covered bridge in Ashland

across the Ottauquechee River with a capstan turned by oxen. He built the bridge for $15,000 less than the estimated cost of a steel bridge.

From Graton's new Ashland bridge, return to US 3 and drive two-tenths of a mile to where a view of the lake opens up. Pull over for a broadside look at Graton's feat and a nice view of the lake.

During the next mile and three-quarters, you'll pass some resort cabins and inns. Note that some of them refer to "Golden Pond." Squam Lake (ahead) was the site of the 1981 movie *On Golden Pond* with Henry Fonda and Katharine Hepburn.

Make sure to stop at the Science Center of New Hampshire, near the junction of US 3 and Route 113 in the center of Holderness. (Immediately before this junction, you'll pass the Science Center Nature Store; return to this later.) Turn left on Route 113, and in one-tenth of a mile, turn left again at the Science Center sign.

Begun in 1966, the Science Center of New Hampshire was designed as a 200-acre outdoor classroom about New Hampshire's plants, animals, and birds. Twenty-five thousand children a year learn about wildlife in a statewide school program at the center. A three-quarter-mile exhibit trail winds through the adjoining woods and fields inhabited by (enclosed) black bears, deer, eagles, raptors, otters, and other local species.

Afterward, stop at the Science Center Nature Store on US 3, a long block back from the Route 113 junction. Upstairs is the Fauver Gallery, with an impressive array of raptors and other birds on display. Downstairs is a wide selection of environmental items for sale, with all the profits going to the Science Center. The store is housed in the old Holderness Inn, which was scheduled for demolition a few years ago.

Continue back on US 3 to the Route 113 junction (you'll see the Holderness Public Library on the corner) and head toward Center Harbor on US 3. For the next four miles, blue flashes of pristine Squam Lake shimmer through the green pines and spruce trees on your left. Now and then, yard sales and flea markets will tempt you with attic treasures among the basement bric-a-brac. Many a deal has been done at these roadside lawn shops. Who knows what good talking and shopping you may find.

Suddenly, Route 25B east appears on your left. Follow this smallish road to Center Harbor, a little more than three miles away. The road meanders through rolling hills with an open field here, rich woodlands there, a hill-ringed swamp on the right, and the Hearthstone Farm and apple orchards on the left. A hand-painted sign on a corner oak reads, "Haste Ye Back."

Soon you're moving downhill, and a stupendous view of Lake Winnipesaukee opens up before you. This tree-lined lake is of one of the largest in-state lakes in the nation. The Nichols Memorial Public Library stands on the right, and the town center fountain flows on the left, but you scarcely see either one. Lake Winnipesaukee dominates the horizon, and from this elevated hillside angle, you get a wonderful view. Center Harbor offers parking spaces on both sides of the street so you can stop for a look before driving closer.

Moultonborough to Castle in the Clouds

From the center of Center Harbor, drive down the short hill to Route 25. At the traffic light, turn left toward Moultonborough. In about a mile and half, look for Moultonborough Neck Road at the top of a hill. This six-and-a-half-mile road takes you onto a peninsula and to a marina, the Moultonborough town beach, and a small bridge with long channels of Lake Winnipesaukee on both sides.

The side trip takes you through woodlands, along some small marshes and fields, and by an updated country store offering lunch supplies for a lakeside bite. You might even see some deer along the way.

When you're close to six miles along, watch for a Y junction. Be sure to veer to the right on Long Island Road. This takes you, in another half mile, to a public access to the lake.

Lake Winnipesaukee forms a ragged patchwork quilt of inlets, coves, islands, and peninsulas—the water centerpiece of New Hampshire. The state is blessed with more than 2,000 lakes and ponds and 40,000 miles of streams. Seeing the grand lake up close gives you a sense of its breadth and beauty. From 1652, when white explorers traced the headwaters of the Merrimack River to The Weirs at the west side of the lake, Winnipesaukee has been a center-stage attraction.

Wide and wonderful Winnipesaukee has always presented a natural opportunity for cruising. The first steamer took to the waters in 1833, but when the elegant and famous *Lady of the Lake* steamer first plied the deep blue water in 1849, the lake grew in popularity and activity. Some projects, such as building a proposed canal from Lake Winnipesaukee to Portsmouth, were ditched. But in 1903, the first YMCA summer camp was started in Wolfeboro, beginning the summer camp movement that continues today.

Follow Moultonborough Neck Road back to Route 25 and turn right. In a little more than three miles, go straight through the Route 109 junction (you'll see the Moultonborough Public Library on the corner). In about one-half mile, the road opens out onto a cattail marsh and an airport. In the distance, you'll see rounded mountain peaks. Take a right on Route 109 south, and in 2.2 miles veer to the left onto Route 171 east to Castle in the Clouds. Watch for the sign.

Working farmers and their gentlemen counterparts live along this two-mile stretch to the entrance to Castle Springs, the new corporate name for the old Castle in the Clouds mansion. The one-way, 1.8-mile entrance road climbs effortlessly up through mountainside woods, by a boulder brook, past "The Pebble" (an outsized, seemingly tottering boulder), and a get-out-of-your-car waterfall to admire. Near the top, a turnout affords a spectacular view of the Lake Winnipesaukee complex.

A tour of Thomas Plant's exotic mansion, which required the work of a thousand Italian stonemasons to build, transports you to an era of extravagant mountaintop living. Today Castle in the Clouds offers equestrian facilities that include eighty-five miles of sumptuous trails and a function room for conferences. Don't forget to take home some samples of Castle Springs water, bottled from the high-country natural springs known by white settlers since the seventeenth century, when these Ossipee Mountains were first explored.

Back at Route 171, turn left toward Moultonboro.

Melvin Village to Wolfeboro

Getting to Melvin Village requires a few nimble turns for the next ten minutes. After passing the Castle Springs entrance, in about one and a half miles, you'll see the sign for Melvin Village, which tells you to turn right onto Sodom Road. One mile later, turn right onto New Road. In three-quarters of a mile, turn right onto County Road. Two-tenths of a mile later, turn left onto High Street, and follow this downhill to the stop sign at Route 109. Voilà! Melvin Village.

This charming village on the lakeshore is a delight. Don't resist the country store, which matches the welcoming simplicity of the village.

Follow Route 109 out of town (*not* Route 109A a mile later) and all the way to Wolfeboro. Some breaks in the woods show Winnipesaukee on the right, but sometimes small blue ponds can be seen on the left, too. About five and a half miles from Melvin Village, Mirror Lake will be on your left, which means you're getting close to the Libby Museum.

When Route 109 suddenly opens onto Winter Harbor, the Libby Museum stands directly opposite you, across the road. A park borders the shore, and it, along with the natural history museum, offers you a place for a well-earned rest.

The museum opened in 1912 in a one-story, classical-style building with the fauna and flora collection of Dr. Henry Forrest Libby. Since then, other collections have been added, including ancient Abenaki artifacts and arrowheads dating back 6,000 to 7,000 years. Birds mounted as if in flight, a 350-year-old dugout canoe, and many other items fill the museum, which mainly houses local wildlife specimens and prehistoric artifacts.

Wolfeboro lies three miles farther on. Before you drive all the way down the hill to the town center, consider taking the cruise from the Wolfeboro Inn, on the right. The inn operates the 65-foot *Judge Sewall* that leaves from the town dock. The cruise takes ninety minutes.

Downtown Wolfeboro, a block away from the lake, offers many cozy shops to explore. Billed as "The Oldest Summer Resort in America," Wolfeboro was the home of John Wentworth II, the third Wentworth family governor of the British colony, who was adept at dealing with the twists and turns of the lumbering laws. Great wealth accumulated in the Wentworth family, much of it through their land acquisitions and ship-masting business for the British Crown. Their political and economic power dominated the colony for sixty years, until the Revolution. The Wentworths gradually lost favor with the Crown in their push to establish townships (including land reserves for their families), which strengthened the New Hampshire colony. John II developed the College Road that led from Wolfeboro to Hanover and Dartmouth College, which he also established.

Alton Bay to Meredith

Follow Route 28 from Wolfeboro toward Alton. In about seven and a half miles, turn right onto Route 28A to Alton Bay.

Eventually, this winds around the shoreline of the southern end of Lake Winnipesaukee for a mile.

Pick up Route 11 to the right, which will take you north toward Weirs Beach. Alton Bay is full of faded reminders of one of the earliest summering settlements on the lake. The first-class cruise ship the *Mount Washington* docks in its narrow, deep cove. Entertainment, a Sunday champagne brunch, and other elegant features highlight this ship, which also docks at Wolfeboro, Weirs Beach, and Center Harbor. Moonlight dinner-dance cruises, as well as daytime cruises, fill the schedule from late June to early September.

Driving along Route 11, you'll see crowded towns and miles of enjoyable countryside. The west side of Lake Winnipesaukee definitely differs from the east.

West Alton, about nine miles north, offers some good water views. Two and a half miles later, turn right onto the Ellacoya State Beach scenic road, which overlaps Belknap Point Road. It hugs the shore for a while, although much commercial concrete has sprouted up between road and lake. A mile and a quarter along, you'll hook up again with Route 11 west.

One and a half miles later, turn right at the traffic light onto Route 11B north. Go straight for a little over three miles to US 3. You'll definitely see the Weirs Beach neon arrow directing you to the center of town. The arrow does not point to the area where early people camped and fished and left their arrowheads thousands of years ago. Instead, you'll see food pavilions, pizzerias, penny arcades, bumper cars, water slides, and other noisy amusements. Consider taking the hourly train ride along the shore to Meredith on the old-time, three-car, whistle-blowing locomotive of the Winnipesaukee & Pemigewasset Valley Railroad.

The five-mile drive up US 3 toward Meredith runs through other fun spots. Turn left onto Route 104, just south of Meredith, and follow it seven miles to I-93.

In the Area

All phone numbers are within area code 603.

Castle in the Clouds–Castle Springs, Moultonborough: 800-729-2468

Judge Sewall cruise, Wolfeboro Inn: 569-3016

Libby Museum, Wolfeboro: 569-1035

Mount Washington cruise, Weirs Beach: 366-2628

Science Center of New Hampshire, Holderness: 968-7194

Winnipesaukee & Pemigewasset Valley Railroad, Weirs Beach: 366-2366

4 ~

Kancamagus
Highway

From Manchester and Concord in the south or **Littleton** in the north: take I-93 to exit 32 at Lincoln. Drive east onto Route 112, the Kancamagus Highway. Approximately 36 miles.

Highlights: *Tunnels of maples, oaks, and beeches, scenic overlooks, Mount Kancamagus, alpine ponds, mountaintop cliffs, Sabbaday and Rocky Gorge falls, the Russell-Colbath House, the Swift River.*

Who Was Kancamagus?

As you turn off I-93, the White Mountain Information Center straight ahead gives you the answer. Chief Kancamagus worked to keep peace between English settlers and Native Americans living in these river valleys and along these mountain slopes. Called "The Fearless One," he was chief of the Penacook Confederacy of seventeen tribes, which his grandfather Passaconaway united in 1627. Precarious relations between the newcomers and the natives eventually forced the tribes north, and by 1691, the tribes had scattered as far away as Canada. To commemorate Kancamagus and his people's contribution to the area, the state officially named the road the Kancamagus Highway in 1961.

A long time in coming, the beloved highway today owes its existence to early white settlers who hacked out tiny plots of farmland from raw but fertile country along the Swift River twelve miles from Conway. They called their settlement Passaconaway, in honor of Kancamagus's grandfather. The road between these two towns became a highway more than a century later.

By 1837, a decent town road was laid down. The big cross-the-range idea grew slowly. In the 1920s, a single-lane unpaved road extended from Conway to Passaconaway on the east side of the mountain passes. In the late 1930s, surveys were made to push a road all the way to Lincoln on the western side. Decades and dedication to the project finally led to an end-to-end road in 1959. In 1964, the two-lane highway was completely paved, though closed in winter. Four years later, guardrails and other safety improvements allowed the road to be opened year-round. In 1989, the Kancamagus Highway was dedicated as a National Scenic Byway.

Lincoln to Kancamagus Pass

This is an enjoyable drive at any time of year, but in autumn, it's spectacular. The gorgeous color along the road during the fall will take your breath away.

Out of Lincoln, head east on the Kancamagus Highway, otherwise known as Route 112. In little more than a mile, Lincoln disappears from sight and mind, and you're soon passing a "Brake for Moose" sign, with a note that about 200 collisions have occurred. If one of these great, gangly animals bursts from the trees, your double duty is, first, not to collide with it, and second, to marvel at the spectacle.

Once past the Loon Mountain ski area, you'll find yourself in the White Mountain National Forest, a U.S. Forest Service reserve. Because of this, the road is free of fast-food restaurants or billboards.

About a mile and a quarter after the ski slopes, an informational turnout on the right tells you something about where you are. Walk down the short slope to the sand-colored boulders sticking up from the East Branch of the Pemigewasset River. The softly cascading water is mountain filtered and as clear as Steuben glass.

Turn left a mile later (immediately after crossing a bridge) into the Lincoln Woods Visitor Information Center, located in a new log cabin. A footbridge over the East Branch of the Pemigewasset, itself a tributary of the broad-shouldered Merrimack River, leads to a walking trail worth exploring. Thick, first-growth forests were logged here from 1890 to 1947, even though the White Mountain National Forest was established in 1925. Lumbering thrived, as a billion board feet of timber was removed by thirty-two logging campsites and seventy-two miles of railroad. Times have changed. Now the White Mountain National Forest and the Appalachian Mountain Club share maintenance of seventy-six miles of foot trails in the forest, one of which you're walking on this trip.

Continue up this gently rising section of the Kancamagus through the woods. In a mile, you'll see Big Rock Campground on the left. Farther on, you'll pass trailheads and rest areas as the road gets a bit steeper.

Cruise along. Pull over and let others pass. You're in no hurry. The highway is only about thirty-six miles long, which gives you ample time to stop the car now and then, sit and relax, or walk a pace or two up a trail.

In a few minutes, the road winds around a horseshoe (or hairpin) turn as it climbs steeper by the mile. Right after this double-back turn is the Hancock Overlook on the right.

Around here, the road angles up to about a nine percent grade, which means that you ascend nine feet for every 100 feet of length—not really that steep going up. After about two and a half miles of this, the Pemi Overlook appears on the left.

The lovely cascade of Sabbaday Falls

As you hook around to the parking area above the highway, the long, downward slope of the mountain valleys to the west makes a wondrous view. Mount Kancamagus rises up straight across from you.

Kancamagus Pass to Sabbaday Falls

Less than one-half mile farther on, you clear Kancamagus Pass at 2,855 feet, the highest point on the road. More of the White Mountain world at Pemi Overlook surrounds you, but it's nice to know you're finally on top of it all.

The next four miles slide downhill at a seven percent grade. The C.L. Graham picnic area comes up on the left in about a tenth of a mile. Tables invite you to stop for a short snack and a long view of the mountains and valleys.

Two and a half miles later, you'll see a small alpine lake that resembles a Japanese garden. Elegant grasses rim the pond. A white earth path leads a few steps down through the brush to the edge of the lake.

Two miles later, the Sugar Hill Overlook offers high drama, especially during the vibrant fall leaf season. The sheer, rocky edge of Green's Cliff juts upward at the extreme left, showing hints of the famed deep notches (gorges) of Pinkham, Crawford, and Franconia. Then straight ahead in the staggered distance, the mountainous humps of Owl Cliff, Three Sisters, and Mount Chocorua fill the high horizon. Take time to see how the Ice Age scraped out the soft guts of the land and left the hard granite to shape the people.

In a little more than two miles, the trail to Sabbaday Falls starts on the right. You can't miss the parking lot. The trail to the Ice Age 11,000 years ago is wide, smooth, and easy on the legs and lungs. A one-way trip takes between five and fifteen minutes. Take twenty if you must, but definitely take the trail.

Nearing the falls, walk to the left of the trail junction. This leads you to the base of the falls—miniature compared to the giants—but you can investigate this one up close. At the top, the white water squeezes through a hard-rock funnel canyon. At the base of the falls, the water pools into a shallow saucer of lustrous, crystalline greens and blues.

Walk up the wooden staircase alongside the falls to the top. There you'll get the reverse line of sight—a cramped, rocky chute down which the energetic water gushes, trying its best to erode the obstruction away.

When the pioneers settled here in the Passaconaway Valley, they first reached these loud-rushing falls on a Sunday, their day off. They returned to the falls on the next Sabbath, and the next, until the weekly trip became known as the "Sabbath Day" trip. Eventually, the falls became known as the Sabbaday Falls.

Once you're back onto the road, enjoy the next three miles, as the terrain flattens out a bit and clearings appear sporadically along the way. It feels as if you're emerging from the mountains and coming to the end of the Kancamagus Highway. But you have much more to see, especially the Russell-Colbath House three miles from the falls.

In 1832, Thomas Russell built this one-and-a-half-story, wood-frame house with a center chimney. The gritty and grizzly Russell operated a sawmill nearby. Records show that he and others hauled lumber to Portland, Maine, which kept the shipbuilding business going, and brought back kegs of rum, which kept the men going. Thomas's son Amzi and his descendants lived in the house until 1930. In 1961, the U.S. Forest Service bought full rights to the house, and in 1987 it was included on the National Register of Historic Places. The building remains as the only nineteenth-century farmstead in the area.

This is a charming site to visit. A small tomato-and-bean garden grows every summer beside the house, and a hostess, dressed in period clothing, mills about hoeing and answering questions. Inside, the four-room house features an outsized spinning wheel, an old-time rocking chair, and a pump organ. The huge stone fireplace, with a granite base, sports cast-iron cookware and herbs and apples drying on a string overhead. If you're lucky, the hostess will tell you this story about Thomas Russell's granddaughter Ruth. One day in 1891, while Ruth was preparing dinner, her husband, Thomas Colbath, went outside, telling his wife as he left, "I'll be back in a little while." When he didn't return in a little while, she ate supper and lit the lamp, placing the light in the window for him to see when he returned. Stalwart and regular, Ruth kept lighting the lamp and placing it in the window every night for thirty-nine years. She died in 1930. Thomas returned in 1933. No Ruth, no lamp.

Passaconaway to Conway

One-half mile from the Russell-Colbath House, the first through road off the Kancamagus Highway exits left. It leads to Bear Notch Road and Bartlett nine miles away. Continue straight ahead to Champney Falls a couple of miles along. It's probably not worth the two-and-a-half-hour round-trip hike to the falls; they're spectacular only in high water. Unless you're traveling during a rainy spring, skip the side trip.

Rocky Gorge lies less than two miles down the road. Here an easy trail over a footbridge leads to the picturesque falls only a short distance away. The Swift River, which you've been paralleling for miles, has smoothed the boulders and left many midriver perches for you too.

Take your time covering the remaining eight and a half miles of the highway. A picnic area less than two miles along offers more boulders in the middle of the river where you can eat your lunch. The Covered Bridge Campground a mile down the road offers another while-away spot.

When you leave the White Mountain National Forest, you'll run directly into Routes 16 and 113 in Conway. Turn left to continue on to North Conway.

In the Area

Both phone numbers are within area code 603.

Loon Mountain, Lincoln: 745-8111

White Mountain National Forest, District Ranger, Conway: 447-5448

5 ~

Mascoma

to

Franklin

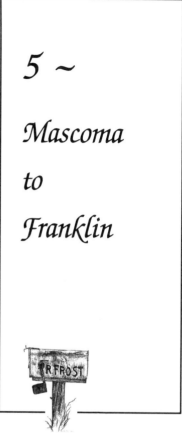

From Concord: Take I-89 north to exit 17, then east on US 4 two miles to Route 4A south. From Brattleboro, Vermont, take I-91 north to exit 10 at White River Junction, Vermont, then I-89 east across the Connecticut River to exit 17, then US 4 east to Route 4A. This trip runs approximately 39 miles.

Highlights: *Mascoma Lake, La Salette Shrine, Lower Shaker Village, country towns, low-lying woodlands, rolling hills, Daniel Webster's birthplace.*

Mascoma to Lower Shaker Village

In the settlement of Mascoma on US 4, take Route 4A south toward the old Shaker Village. In less than one-half mile, you'll arrive at the narrow, fingertip top of Mascoma Lake, where houses line the shore. A mile farther on, after a turn in the road, you'll suddenly come upon a long view of the full breadth of the lake. A bridge spans the last of the narrows, and in three-quarters of a mile, you can take a short side tour on the other side of the bridge. Actually, the bridge gives you lift enough for an encompassing view of the wider section of the lake, its calm surface spreading far and away.

During the next mile, you'll pass the lakeside Shaker Bridge Motel, a cemetery slanting downhill in the distance to the left, a summer produce stand, a house built in 1804, the white Community Lutheran Church on the left, and, uphill a bit, the Enfield Public Library, located in a turreted, remodeled Victorian home. Enfield remains a living, working small country town.

Cross back over the bridge, and before you know it, Route 4A opens onto La Salette Shrine and Lower Shaker Village. The shrine comes first, on your right.

This dual complex originally included only the old Shaker community (1793–1923) that devoted its life and legacy to the religious convictions of founder Mother Ann. La Salette missionaries bought the property in 1927 and founded a seminary here. After the seminary closed, the La Salettes maintained the shrine. And on the property today, you'll find an inn and restaurant and a nonprofit museum.

Explore the hillside peacefulness of the shrine. Built in 1951, it is modeled on the shrine at La Salette, France, that commemorates the apparition of Mary, the Mother of Jesus, in 1846. Walks are well laid out and sculptures artistically displayed. The top of the hill affords a fine view of the lake and some of the remaining Shaker buildings, including the gift shop at the shrine.

Driving across Route 4A, you can't miss two large stone buildings—a Greco-Roman chapel and the Great Stone Dwelling. Complete with Mediterranean stone pillars inside and out and sumptuous stained glass windows, the Mary Keane Chapel jars the eye and heart after the restful simplicity of the Shakers. The Great Stone Dwelling was built with precision and patience by the Shakers themselves in 1837 as the separate but equal dwelling place of the community. It's now the Shaker Inn.

Behind these buildings (you can drive around them and park) lies the Museum at Lower Shaker Village, which offers this Shaker version of the No Smoking sign: "All persons are Forbid using Tobacco in This House."

A map and brochures lead you on a self-guided tour of the grounds. One of the original Shaker buildings next to the museum is an 1854 barn, with an earth ramp angling up to the second floor. The restaurant at the Shaker Inn (in the Great Stone Dwelling) includes a Shaker-style, peg-rail dining room (with Shaker chairs, to be sure) and Shaker-inspired food.

A sense of decorum and efficiency translated to every aspect of living the Shaker life, especially the furniture. "Trifles make perfection, but perfection is no trifle" remains a legacy carried on today by the Dana Robes Wood Craftsmen, located in a neighboring building. Shaker chairs, tables, and doors are crafted here by hand and offered for sale in the showroom, open year-round.

Enfield Center to Wilmot

For the next seventeen miles or so on Route 4A, the world of pizza parlors and parking lots gives way to a country road of simpler sights. You'll pass a white-fenced horse farm, scattered houses, a fruit stand here, a vegetable stand there. In three miles, you'll enter Enfield Center: Union Church on the left, 1843 Town House on the right, 1851 Historical Society Museum in a reconverted church. This road-hugging town lives a sturdy two-century life.

Soon you're on to a slight upgrade as the wooded roadway passes a lily-pad-infested appendage of George Pond on the left. You can't miss the one-story barn from the old days, when summer haying was central to winter survival.

On you cruise. Take your time. Enjoy this next four-mile stretch as Route 4A develops into a straight and narrow road.

Houses are scattered along the route, where neighbors mean pileated woodpeckers and raccoons. As you go downhill, you'll see a cattail swamp on the left.

Two and a quarter miles after you pass the Abenaki Timber Corp. sign on the right, stop at the nameless pond on the left. It's small, peaceful, and open. Some oak stumps along the edge of the pond provide a place for you to sit and enjoy the view.

Continue along through the Giles State Forest for a couple of miles until you come to a curve. A little beyond is the Gardner Memorial Wayside Park, on the left, a charming, one-table picnic spot. Turn in for a snack, lunch, or stretch. Take a short walk across the tree-shaded boulder brook gurgling below the footbridge.

One-tenth of a mile farther down the road, a marker notes one of the earliest land grants in the New World. In 1629, the English Crown bestowed on Captain John Mason a huge tract of land bounded on the west and north by a curved line sixty miles from the Atlantic. From this parcel evolved townships, estates, and other land patents, with this original proprietary boundary as the point of reference. Called the Masonian Curve, the boundary coincides with the town line between Springfield and Wilmot. It also signifies that Wilmot lies only about five miles away in increasingly undulating country.

Established in 1807, Wilmot today is a well-painted, well-shaded small town alongside Kimpton Brook, companion also to Route 4A for many miles. Be sure to turn left onto North Wilmot Road, the first street as you enter the core of the town. Directly ahead stands the old town center—three white buildings in a row: Town Hall and Grange, Wilmot Public Library, church with horse-and-buggy stalls. This is a town of poetry and classical music. Take a look, and savor the memory when you leave for wider asphalt and concrete.

Continue following Route 4A south. One last curve two miles away opens onto a lovely view of flat-top Mount

Kearsarge ahead. One-half mile or so later, turn left onto Route 11 east at the stop sign.

Andover and Daniel Webster's Birthplace

As you head for Andover on Route 11 (*not* West Andover and the Ragged Mountain Ski Area), turn right at the Potter Place sign for a half-mile detour to this settlement, all but a village memory. The Potter Place Inn and Restaurant is a welcoming stop. A rejuvenated railroad car and railroad train station (now the Andover Historical Society Museum) stand across the way. This glimpse of yesteryear is named after Richard Potter, who died here in 1835 on his estate. Potter was a magician, ventriloquist, and showman who wowed American audiences as "Master of the Black Arts."

The next stretch of Route 11 between Andover, incorporated in 1779, and East Andover is a transition and not much else. Once out of Andover, be sure to turn left onto Route 11

*Birthplace of
Daniel Webster*

east (*not* US 4 east, straight ahead) for half a dozen miles to East Andover. Once you pass a cemetery on the left as you're about to curve into East Andover, the countryside grows more appealing. Highland Lake to your left becomes visible as you drive up toward the white church at the top of the hill.

Immediately before the church, turn left over a wooden bridge and continue past a lake inlet, old shoreline houses, weeping willows, red maples, inns, and furniture makers. Drive straight on a while, then turn around and park your car in the visitors lot at the corner of the first street near the wooden bridge. Walk along the inlet and soak up the scenery.

Daniel Webster was born in backcountry New Hampshire, and that's where you're going next.

From East Andover, return across the wooden bridge to the hilltop church on Route 11. Turn right on Route 11, going back the way you came. Pass the post office on the left toward the curve on Route 11; the curve is less than one-half mile away. Go straight ahead onto Flaghole Road. Watch the traffic. Daniel Webster's birthplace is 4.2 miles along on Flaghole Road.

In six-tenths of a mile, turn left at the first junction. The road may appear to be heading into the wilderness, but relax and enjoy the quiet stretches and working farms along the way. Proceed uphill into high cornfield country. At 1.8 miles, turn right at the second junction. A mile later, you're heading down into the trees again, winding along. At 4.2 miles from Route 11, you'll come to a clearing, with Daniel Webster's dark brown birth cabin straight ahead and a white farmhouse to the side.

This state historic site commemorates frontier life and the stupendous human spirit that can emerge from unpolished beginnings. Take a tour of the place. Climb the wooden stairs for a peek at the attic bedroom where the children slept on corn-husk mattresses. The cabin is outfitted with original and replicated furnishings, including a cradle, cast-iron toasters,

waffle makers, foot warmers, the original floors, and a fireplace.
Daniel Webster (1782–1852) served America for forty years as a U.S. representative from both New Hampshire and Massachusetts (he moved to Marshfield, Massachusetts, later in life). He was secretary of state under three presidents and ran for president himself.

The fourth, feeble child of Ebenezer and Abigail Webster, Daniel astounded his elders and teachers with his knowledge and memorization of the Bible and works of English literature. He came from sturdy New England stock—four generations of Websters had worked the soil before him. He inherited his father's sense of drama and his mother's love of reading, and he became a celebrated orator, earning the title "Defender of the Constitution."

When he opened a law practice in Marshfield, Massachusetts, he said of New Hampshire, "For my part, I shall continue to love her white-topped hills, her clear running streams, her beautiful lakes, and her deep shady forests, as long as I live."

Continue downhill for three-quarters of a mile to the stop sign at Route 127. Turn left toward Franklin. Go two more miles or so, and you'll come to the junction of US 3.

In the Area

All phone numbers are within area code 603.

Dana Robes Wood Craftsmen, Enfield: 632-5385

Daniel Webster's Birthplace, Franklin: 934-5057 in summer; 271-3254 off-season

La Salette Shrine, Enfield: 632-7087

Lower Shaker Village, Enfield: 632-4346

Shaker Inn, Enfield: 632-7800

6 ~

Derry to
Durham

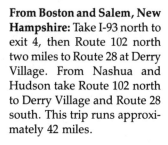

From Boston and Salem, New Hampshire: Take I-93 north to exit 4, then Route 102 north two miles to Route 28 at Derry Village. From Nashua and Hudson take Route 102 north to Derry Village and Route 28 south. This trip runs approximately 42 miles.

Highlights: *Robert Frost's farm, Stonehenge on Mystery Hill, Kingston, Phillips Exeter Academy, the Great Bay tidal basin, University of New Hampshire.*

Derry Village and the Robert Frost Farm

At the rotary in Derry Village, two miles east of Derry, swing onto Bypass Route 28 south to the Robert Frost Farm, 1.7 miles straight down this road. You'll pass the Derry Village School on the left in one-half mile. Another one-half mile along, the straight-ahead road changes to Route 28 south (not the bypass). You'll soon come to the farm on the left.

Don't be dismayed by the body of the farm; its spirit has enriched our nation far beyond what the eye can see. The farm memorializes many of Robert Frost's important works.

This state historic site maintains the bare-white simplicity of Frost's early years. The farmhouse, where four of Frost's children grew up, stands close to the road, its small rooms testimony to rural life at the turn of the century. The connecting barn contains memorabilia of Frost's life (1874–1963), and the soft, slanting field behind evokes the seeds of poems that he long ago harvested and that have endured.

Early on, Frost himself recognized that he could grow verse better than potatoes. In fact, all New Hampshire became his poetic fields. His first book, *A Boy's Will* (at age forty), sprang from this Derry farm. His second, *North of Boston*, revolves around New Hampshire characters. *Mountain Interval* refers to the land around his later farm in Franconia, *New Hampshire* makes it plain enough where his nourishment lay, and *West Running Brook* takes its title from the stream that flows through Derry.

Frost owned the Derry farm for nine years. When he sold it to help finance his adventure into metaphors and meter, the farm and its neighbors remained with him. His Derry connections traveled with him to London, where his first two books were published. When he returned to the States, his reputation had blossomed where his roots had sunk.

Reputation gave him tang. What was his answer to annoying questions of what he did in the woods? "Gnaw bark." Why did he want to return to New Hampshire and live in Franconia? "Live cheap and get Yankier and Yankier."

Frost dropped out of Dartmouth as a freshman, getting his poetic license later. He won the Pulitzer Prize four times, in 1921, 1931, 1937, and 1943. He received an Honorary Doctor of Letters from Dartmouth in 1933 and an Honorary Doctor of Laws from Dartmouth in 1955.

Some of his most cherished poems derive from his Derry farm, including "Mending Wall" and "Birches." New Hampshire counties appear in "The Pauper Witch of Grafton" and "The Witch of Coos." Town names such as Andover,

Colebrook, Dublin, Franconia, Littleton, and Windham color his poems. Frost once said, "Nearly half of my poems must actually have been written in New Hampshire." And after listing all his Granite State connections, he added, "So you see it has been New Hampshire, New Hampshire with me all the way."

North Salem and America's Stonehenge

From Derry Village, head south on Route 28 toward North Salem, where Major General John Stark's birthplace is acknowledged 2.4 miles from the Frost farm. During the early years of the American resistance to British colonization, Stark commanded the New Hampshire Minutemen in Massachusetts. A year after the Declaration of Independence, Stark's men defeated two British detachments under General John Burgoyne near Bennington, Vermont, on August 16, 1777. Two months later, Burgoyne surrendered, marking the first great American victory of the Revolution.

After you breech a hill and pass the Windham Motel five miles later, you'll soon come to the junction of Route 111. Turn left onto Route 111 east. One-half mile along, you'll see a lake on the left, which will stay with you almost a mile before the open road takes over.

Three and a half miles after turning onto Route 111, you'll see the sign "America's Stonehenge. Prehistoric Site 1 Mile" on the right. Turn right, continuing straight through the stop sign in two-tenths of a mile. In little more than a quarter mile, veer to the right. Four-tenths of a mile later is the entrance to America's Stonehenge.

Once called Mystery Hill, America's Stonehenge stimulates one's archaeological imagination. A private research station, this twenty-acre site offers self-guided tours and a map that take you through a series of baffling configurations and arrangements of standing stones. The four-ton Sacrificial

Table, grooved around the perimeter to drain blood, perches on stone legs. Beneath the table lies the Speaking Tube from the Oracle Chamber. Roof slabs, a sump pit, wall ruins, and water channels are evident.

Who lived here? Who made these chambers? Who moved the giant stones? Theories have proliferated since their discovery in 1823. Two series of research reports are intriguing. In 1969, carbon dating analyzed in Cambridge, Massachusetts, determined that charcoal found at an excavation site dated the spot at 3,000 years old. The following year, a second carbon-14 analysis dated the site at almost 4,000 years old.

That same year, a closer examination of peripheral standing stones in relation to the central site showed a correlation with elaborate astronomical alignments. Those who had built the site had determined exact equinoxes and solstices, in addition to pointing toward exact moonrises, sunsets, and midseason alignments of certain stars. Tools and ancient European linguistic scripts found on the site add to the mystery of this hill.

Kingston and Exeter

From America's Stonehenge, return to Route 111 east, which takes you on an open, easy drive. You'll pass ponds now and then, and a swamp or two. Take in the gentle countryside. Stay on Route 111 all the way to Kingston (don't be tempted by Route 111A).

In eight and a half miles, the road narrows as you enter Kingston. Turn left at a stop sign, and you'll soon see the Kingston Town Beach on the left. Continue on to Kingston State Park, about a mile away.

This 44-acre, day-use state park shines like a gem. The Civilian Conservation Corps (CCC) helped develop the simple but engaging park from 1933 to 1942. The curved sandy beach, separate picnic area on small hilltops or in Clark's

Hollow, an isolated section of West Hill around the bend from the main beach, and tall spruce and pine trees make this a nice place to rest and recreate.

Directly opposite the park entrance begins the half-mile-long Kingston green, bordered by a two-lane road on both sides. The common invites a slow drive around it. Note especially the Kingston 1686 House, a fine restaurant on the east side, and the twice-as-tall-as-wide Kingston Country Store at the northern end.

Josiah Bartlett practiced medicine here for forty-five years, experimenting with quinine for malaria in the second half of the eighteenth century. He was one of three New Hampshire men to sign the Declaration of Independence and the Articles of Confederation, and he was the first man to hold the title of governor of New Hampshire. A marker in Bartlett's memory stands on the green.

In its early years, Kingston was famous for its bog iron. Ore was dug from nearby swamps and smelted over intensely hot charcoal made from hardwood. Chopping wood was big business at the time; it took an estimated 6,000 cords a year to keep a typical iron furnace going.

Don't miss the Nichols Memorial Library across the way from the general store. Made of stone, the library features arabesque detailing over its heavy wooden door hung on massive hinges, a ceiling lined with wood, windows of stained glass, and a granite fireplace elaborately carved with these words: "This building was erected by J. Howard Nichols, a native of this town, in loving remembrance of his parents Nicholas and Mary Barstow Nichols. MDCCCX-CVIII."

For the next six miles, Route 111 winds through dense and then open country. On the outskirts of Exeter, you'll come to a triangular island in the road with an historic marker identifying this as the "Revolutionary Capital." Veer to the right of this island.

Along with Portsmouth, Hampton, and Dover, Exeter was one of the first four towns of New Hampshire. Until the Revolution, these towns reigned as the supreme economic and political settlements. Exeter was proud of its property-

Kingston Country Store

owning Puritans, who fought the royal authority for whatever political opportunity they could get. Townspeople grew increasingly cantankerous and independent as 1776 approached. The General Court Assembly was made up of leaders who inexorably thumbed their noses at the royal governor. As they moved further away from the king and toward the service of the people, they held secret opposition sessions in Exeter, away from the royal governorship in Portsmouth. When the Revolution began, Exeter was chosen as New Hampshire's capital. The first New Hampshire State Constitution is dated as follows: "In Congress at Exeter, January 5th, 1776."

The American Independence Museum is located at One Governors Lane off the central campus area. Comprised of the 1721 Ladd-Gilman House and the 1775 Folsom Tavern next door, the museum is permeated with both physical and moral history. Once the home of Governor John Taylor Gilman (1753–1828)m as well as being the treasury when Exeter was the state capital, the museum features three-hundred-year-old furniture and artifacts.

You'll see draft copies of the U.S. Constitution and an original, printed Dunlap Broadside copy of the Declaration of Independence. One of the most prized treasures of the museum is the model for its symbol—the Purple Heart. Three purple hearts were awarded for distinguished service during the American Revolution, and one of them, bestowed on Sgt. Daniel Bissell of Windsor, Connecticut, is part of the collection. The Purple Heart Badge for Military Merit was issued by Gen. George Washington in 1782 when he said: "Whenever any singularly meritorious action is performed, the author of it shall be permitted to wear on his facings, over his left breast, the figure of a heart in purple cloth or silk, edged with narrow lace or binding. Not only instances of unusual gallantry, but also of extraordinary fidelity and essential service in any way should meet with a due reward."

In the heart of Exeter, you'll find a chocolate shop, a soup and bread café, and other small stores. When leaving town, turn right onto Route 108 north, bend around the town center, and then suffer the strip of fast-food restaurants and the like for about a mile. Go straight under the bridge, staying on Route 108 (don't take Route 51 to Hampton).

Soon you're back into fields and farmland. About two and a quarter miles from the bridge, prepare for a rotary; veer left and then right, following Route 108 toward Newmarket. In another five miles or so, you'll see some enchanting tidal marshes to the right and pass over a steel bridge or two. Then you're in Newmarket, with its old brick-and-granite mill buildings beside the Lamprey River.

If you wish to see a secluded section of Great Bay, you'll have to wind around a bit. About one-half mile from Newmarket center, you'll cross a steel bridge with an old dam complex on the right and a tree-lined river scene on the left. A sign proclaiming "Moody Point on Great Bay" signals a quick right. Go up a short grade, then take another quick right. A little over one-half mile past the unkempt back of old buildings, you'll see the entrance to Moody Point. Veer to the right. Drive slowly through this 167-acre residential community, designed as an environmentally protected area. Occasional signs on upright stone slabs instruct you on visitors' use of the area, with stern warnings about abiding by the rules. The goal is to disturb the wildlife habitat as little as possible. Great Bay and its immediate environs constitute a fragile but vital tidal marsh ebbing and flowing as the earth turns. The tides flood and drain Great Bay through the Piscataqua River at Portsmouth harbor. This ancient twice-daily event feeds the shellfish in the muck and the fishing and nesting birds in the air, not to mention the grasses and neighboring shoreline.

Upright stones with signs also mark trails to view Great Bay. One of the best of these trails begins at the end loop of a planned residential street (with few residences built). Walk down the trail on the left, through the grass and into the woods. Follow the wide, cleared path a few yards, and you'll see Great Bay through the trees. Benches are provided on the edge of the woods, and signs suggest that you be as quiet as possible.

When you return to Route 108 north, the road will continue through sections of the seacoast outskirts of Newmarket. In about four miles, a sign on the left marks the turn to Packer's Falls, 1.6 miles west on a country road. This pleasant detour passes by some old-time, back-road farmhouses once you cross the railroad bridge. The road winds mostly through woods until you reach the falls on the Lamprey River.

The turnoff allows one or two cars at a time to visit. A very short walk takes you to the falls, which are really a long cascade that tumbles the Lamprey over steps of boulders with intervening pools.

Once you're back on Route 108 north, just follow it a couple of miles to Durham, home of the main campus of the University of New Hampshire.

In the Area

All phone numbers are within area code 603.

America's Stonehenge, North Salem: 893-8300 or 432-2530

Kingston 1686 House: 642-3637

Phillips Exeter Academy: 772-4311

Robert Frost Farm, Derry Village: 432-3091

University of New Hampshire, Durham: 862-1234

7 ~

Groveton-to-Groveton Circle

From Berlin: Take Route 110 north to Groveton. From Concord take I-93 north through Franconia Notch in the White Mountains to Littleton, then Route 116 north to Route 142 north to US 3 north through Whitefield and Lancaster to Groveton. Approximately 85 miles.

Highlights: *The Balsams, Lake Gloriette, Dixville Notch, Lake Umbagog, the Androscoggin River, White Mountain valleys.*

Groveton to Colebrook

As the miles wheel away on this circular route, the countryside grows better and better. US 3 heading north from Groveton turns narrow but eminently drivable a couple of miles out of town as you head for Colebrook. Much of this early section is rural residential, with occasional dairy farms and gray, weathered barns that have seen better days. The men and women here match this hardy countryside. This is forested land, with a logging history that goes with it.

Every spring around the turn of the century, white-water men rode caravans of logs—poking, spearing, and shoving packs of powerful tree trunks—down the Connecticut River, brimming over with winter snowmelt. They were driving the timber from these high New Hampshire forests to lumber mills down south. The job was a way of life. Today these rugged loggers herd the logs in monstrous cherry-picker trucks, but the woodland spirit of rough work lingers on.

At North Stratford, veer right on US 3 toward Colebrook. In half a dozen miles or so, the terrain flattens out, the sights lengthen, and the farms bend and droop less. You'll notice the difference, and you'll see more of the Connecticut River across the dairy farm fields.

As you approach Colebrook, the Rippling Brook Gift and Craft Shop on the left invites you in. This small family-owned store is located next to the Columbia Town Hall, established in 1770. The shop makes smooth, bright sleighs out back, shipping them all over the country.

A short way ahead, the Shrine of Our Lady of Grace, with an outdoor altar and alcoves for meditating, spans the road. Drive in for a look.

Two miles farther on, you're in Colebrook. For a rest and stretch, take a meal at Howard's Restaurant on Main Street. While you're waiting for your homemade soup and cheeseburger plate (or your homemade cinnamon muffins, doughnuts, mile-high meringue pies, or fudge), consider the following side trip.

Optional Side Trip to Pittsburg

Colebrook acts as a stepping-off point up US 3 to Pittsburg and the source of the Connecticut River. The drive requires at least forty-five miles one way, and you have to return by the same route. But it takes you through Pittsburg, the northernmost town in the state, and on to the Canadian border. The three Connecticut Lakes near the border are linked by expanding rivers, which eventually widen into the full-fledged Connecticut River.

The vast area that Pittsburg now encompasses at the arrowhead tip of New Hampshire was known, in the early nineteenth century, as Indian Stream, a town that once seceded from the United States. After the Revolution, the boundaries of New Hampshire depended on who talked about the boundaries. At this time, nobody knew for certain the northernmost origin of the Connecticut River, which served as the border between New Hampshire and Vermont and the border between New Hampshire and Canada (as part of the Treaty of Paris of 1783). The contested section became known as the Indian Stream Territory, named after one of the three disputed river heads (the others were Halls Stream and Perry Stream).

Disgusted with the territorial limbo, fifty-nine residents of this region, led by Luther Parker, voted 56–3 to form the United Inhabitants of the Indian Stream Republic, with a written constitution, preamble, bill of rights, dictates for a governing assembly, and militia (of forty-one men).

For eight years, the Indian Stream Republic held its own against Canada and the United States—even against its own internal factions. In the end, the New Hampshire legislature sent a state militia of fifty men north to seize the 100,000-acre republic. Two years later the ornery secessionists allowed their territory to be incorporated as the Town of Pittsburg.

In 1842, Daniel Webster and Lord Ashburton of Great Britain worked out the boundary of New England. The U.S. Senate ratified the plan and settled the inflated border of New Hampshire (Webster's home state) at Halls Stream.

The Balsams and Dixville Notch

Pick up Route 26 in the center of Colebrook and drive east to the mountains. The Mohawk River beside you cuts a winding course, flowing in the opposite direction. Your course winds, too. Steep mountains undulate on the horizon as you rise gradually in elevation.

The land opens up, making more of the chunky mountains visible. In ten miles, you're at the entrance to the Balsams Wilderness ski slopes on the right. In winter, the

complex of ski trails covers one peak after another of Dixville Notch. Every year, more than 250 inches of snow blanket the area.

In one-half mile, a wonderful view of the Balsams Grand Resort Hotel appears on the other side of Lake Gloriette. The narrow road curves through the "lobby" of the notch and

Balsams Grand
Resort Hotel

hugs a mountainside on the right. Set at the base of pine-covered mountains, some with sheer rock-face cliffs, the Balsams shows off its evolution of annexes and additions—red-tile roofs, clay-colored walls, sugar-white façades.

Shortly after this glorious scene, turn left at the hotel entrance. Proceed down the road, stopping again at a turnout for another enchanting view of the resort complex, with its circular flower garden, rich green lawn, Olympic-size pool, and deep blue lake.

If you've never visited an updated resort hotel, stroll the grounds and lobbies of this one. Its current 215 rooms and suites have grown from a 25-room guest house established in 1866. The hotel was named the Dix House, after Timothy Dix, the original land grant holder.

In 1897, new owner Henry Hale renamed the hotel the Balsams and built a six-story addition, the first concrete-and-steel structure in New Hampshire. At the dedication of the 120-room Hampshire House, as the addition was called, the music was provided by none other than John Philip Sousa.

Today the veranda, European sitting room, 500-seat dining room, 27-hole golf course, red-clay tennis courts, Ladies' Boutique, Silversmith Shop, and resident artists all add a touch of elegance to the resort.

Once back on Route 26, you'll come to Dixville Notch State Park in a tenth of a mile. The road goes through a short, tight gorge of rocky mountain footings. The high point, at only 1,871 feet, comes soon; and before you know it, you're heading down on a 10 percent grade for another half mile.

You might find the name Dixville Notch vaguely familiar. This minuscule town is the first to report its results in the New Hampshire presidential primaries. Voters usually number only two dozen or so, but woe to the presidential hopeful who does not take pains to stop at Dixville Notch.

Errol and the Androscoggin River

When you leave Dixville Notch State Park, only about a mile and a half long on Route 26, the road levels and the driving turns luxurious. You'll find yourself moving over increasingly open terrain, with mountains in the distance. The North Woods Gift Shop hugs the open road near Millsfield. This is followed by isolated houses and fields, which crowd closer together on the outskirts of Errol.

The backcountry town of Errol sets you to thinking about who lives here, what they do, and where they go. It's a junction type of town. Two of its three roads lead to Maine, not far away. One of these roads—Route 16 north—begins at the far end of what can only be Main Street.

Follow Route 16 for less than two miles along a finger of Lake Umbagog. After the first half mile, the road follows on the heels of the lake for a mile or so. A boat access at 1.6 miles is a good place to pull over for a picnic. In two-tenths of a mile more, the road veers away from the lake, but near here a long, narrow view of the water hints at the lake's size. You're looking east, where the lake spills into Maine.

Backtrack on Route 16 to the stop sign in Errol, turn right, roll through town again, and turn left onto Route 16 south to Milan and Berlin. In about two miles, the Androscoggin River appears on the left. The fingertip of Lake Umbagog you just paralleled gives birth to this river.

Now you're in for a treat—the 13 Miles Woods. Route 16 south follows the river for miles on end, most of them open to this untarnished, slow flow of river, with white water over low-lying boulders periodically sparking the scene.

You'll have plenty of opportunities to pull over, park, and step down the shallow riverbank for a closer look at this ancient river, which has contributed to the lumber industry in Berlin and Gorham, farther downriver. In summer, people fishing in the river complete a perfect picture as they whip their delicate lines overhead. Canoeists lose themselves in reverie paddling along with the grandfatherly pace of the current, then are suddenly caught up in short bursts of excitement when they run the rapids.

At last, the gentle river splits from the road. Three miles later it reappears, offering scenes of backwater marshes and big swamps. Two miles farther along, the Pontook Reservoir Dam works the river on the left. Below the dam, white water perks up the landscape again.

A mile later comes a right turn on Route 110A south to West Milan.

West Milan to Groveton

The four-mile connecting road from Route 16 to West Milan leads through woods, past Cedar Park Campground on Cedar Lake about halfway, and then to Route 110 west. Turn right at the stop sign to head back to Groveton.

Count on the next six miles to Stark for more pleasant country driving—easy road, open land, mountains in the distance, hills up close, and lots of road tag with the Upper Ammonoosuc River.

If you were driving through here between 1944 and 1946, warnings would be posted about the danger of picking up strangers, who could be German or Austrian prisoners of war. Camp Stark, one of nearly 400 such camps in the U.S. and the only one in New Hampshire, held 250 enemy soldiers captured in North Africa and Normandy. The prisoners cut wood for the Brown Paper Company, which was producing plywood, pulp, and other wood products for the war effort.

To make the prison, a former Civilian Conservation Corps (CCC) camp was converted into the POW guardhouse, with high wire fences and four guard towers. The prisoners were sent home after the war, but some of them returned to

Stark for a reunion with their American civilian foremen and guards in 1986.

Stark village lies over a hill, announced by a white church and covered bridge. This tranquil town was established in 1774. About seven more miles of easy driving complete the loop in Groveton.

In the Area

All phone numbers are within area code 603.

Balsams Grand Resort Hotel, Dixville Notch: 255-3400 or 800-678-8946

Howard's Restaurant, Colebrook: 237-4025

North Woods Gift Shop, Millsfield: 482-3205

Rippling Brook Gift and Craft Shop, Colebrook: 237-5753

8 ~

Franconia
Notch

From Manchester and Concord: Take I-93 north past North Woodstock and Lincoln into the White Mountains. The interstate leads directly into Franconia Notch Parkway. This trip runs approximately 19 miles.

Highlights: *Franconia Notch, the Flume, the Basin, Boise Rock, Profile Lake, the Old Man of the Mountain, the Robert Frost Place.*

The Flume

Two wonders dominate celebrated Franconia Notch. The first is the extraordinary gorge. The second lies in the equally extraordinary preservation of this singular canyon while nimbly providing access to it for two million people a year.

A generation ago, developers and engineers planned to continue I-93 full force through the tight valley floor, bulldozing through the notch to lay down four lanes, four shoulders, center aisle, and buffer zones. Fortunately, proponents of goals wider than an interstate highway marshaled the considerable forces of home-state environmentalists and other lovers of the New Hampshire landscape. Led by the *New Hampshire Times*, the Society for the Protection of New Hampshire Forests, and other respected voices, two factions for improving access to Franconia Notch cooked up a compromise. Instead of saddling the notch with a full-fledged interstate highway and its attendant horrors, they proposed building a parkway instead. This also prevented the possible destruction of the fragile Old Man of the Mountain, symbol of New Hampshire.

What you see and drive along today—the Franconia Notch State Parkway—has become an enlightened, practical roadway that retains the splendor of the entire notch. The speed limit is 45 mph. No left turns. Single lane. No passing. No stopping. Turnoffs only at designated sites.

Notice the unobtrusive, quietly sculptured parkway as you enter the notch from I-93 north. In a minute or two, exit 1 announces the turnoff to the Flume. Be sure to stop here.

In the parking lot, a mountain ambiance surrounds you at the new Flume Visitor Center. If you're not among the 180,000 a year who walk through the Flume, be at least among the half million who visit the center. Many interesting museum-style cases display artifacts related to the notch, including a scaled-down model of the Bath covered bridge, maps, and old-time logging equipment.

An authentic Concord Coach catches the eye. This particular stagecoach, #431, carried mail and passengers between Plymouth, New Hampshire, and the Profile House resort a few miles farther north in the notch, making its last run in 1911. The Concord Coach, made in Concord, New Hampshire, between 1826 and 1900 by Abbott, Downing & Co., reigned as the supreme stagecoach of the era and found its way to many other countries. Here you can examine the coach's suspension system, the iron-wrapped, wood-spoke wheels, and the leather-encased spring seats.

Be sure to watch the excellent fifteen-minute video in the Visitor Center Auditorium introducing Franconia Notch. Narrated by Richard Kiley, the video traces the 400-million-year history of the notch, which is older than the Rockies and the Himalayas. You'll also learn about the recent triumph in preserving the basic features of the area. The video prepares you for appreciating the commitment and work that have prevented the notch from being turned into an unrestricted commercial enterprise zone.

The Flume holds sway above all else at this stop. Discovered in 1808, it rises ninety feet, with only twelve to twenty feet between two granite walls. Loud water tumbles through the gorge, misting sun-shy flowers, ferns, and mosses.

A bus drives you halfway to the Flume, or you can walk the seven-tenths of a mile. A fascinating loop trail takes you through two covered bridges, alongside The Pool (a lavish glacier-gouged bowl of water 40 feet deep and 150 feet in diameter), and huge boulders. A boardwalk takes you up inside the gorge. The powerful walls, moistened by the constant spray of the waterfall, press upon you. Being here gives you a true sense of the size and scale of the geological forces that have shaped the earth.

The Basin and Boise Rock

Before moving on, let's address the question about the use of the word "notch." When the early settlers arrived in the New World, they had to build their own houses and other buildings out of logs. To fell trees for log homes, they first axed V's at the base of tree trunks. To shape their cabins true and steady at the four corners, they cut V's or U's in the logs to fit them over each other. They referred to these V's and U's as notches. When the settlers moved farther inland, they discovered deep gorges and canyons in the White Mountains and elsewhere. The gorges looked like V's and U's, so the settlers also referred to them as notches. The name stuck.

The gorgeous gorge of Franconia Notch offers many spectacles, including the Appalachian Trail. On your way to the Basin, you might see the sign announcing the trail, which is just about all you'll see of it. Knowing a little about this great trail may add to your appreciation of Franconia Notch. The Appalachian Trail stretches 2,034 miles through fourteen states from Georgia to Maine. An estimated four million hikers travel some part of this famous trail every year. Scarcely more than a 1,000 have hiked the trail end to end in one season. These thru-hikers, as they're called, might be seen looking straight-ahead and determined as they cross under the parkway, with their legs of iron, wills of steel, and appetites greater than an Illinois threshing machine. In New Hampshire, the Appalachian Trail runs for 154 miles over many of the peaks and ridgelines of the White Mountains, including the bald-topped Presidential Range.

Benton MacKaye conceived the idea of a footpath through the Appalachian Mountains in 1900. By 1922, the first mile had been cut in New York. The last mile was cut in Maine only fifteen years later, in 1937. This granddaddy of all hiking trails enjoys state and federal protection under the National Scenic Trails Act and has given serious and casual hikers countless hours of vigor, pleasure, and communion with nature.

About one-half mile up the parkway, a tantalizing scene on the left side of the notch looms ahead. But first, turn off, as the sign directs another mile ahead, to the Basin, a multiple wonder on a more intimate scale.

Park your car to walk the short distance under the parkway and into the lush woods. The white-water sound you hear and see comes from the Pemigewasset River, whose source you'll be visiting at Profile Lake a few miles up the notch. This river drains Franconia Notch, absorbs tributaries downriver, and eventually merges with the great Merrimack River.

The short path through the woods is shaded by yellow birches, maples, and oaks—the kind of mixed woods inhabited by white-tailed deer, red foxes, hares, raccoons, weasels, bobcats, fishers, Canadian lynx, moose, and black bears.

The Basin itself cradles Pemigewasset water in a bowl thirty feet in diameter, and fifteen feet deep, which looks like a huge emerald sliced in half. The scooped-out pothole, as some call it, developed from receding glacial action in the Ice Age 25,000 years ago.

Mountain water cascades over a short rock bed, its velvety luster the result of endless burnishing. The water itself runs spectacularly clear, a glistening display of purity. No wonder Henry David Thoreau, in his first trip to the White Mountains in 1839, praised the Basin.

About a mile and a half north of the Basin, the notch squeezes the parkway tighter. The mountains rise higher, it seems, and their rockiness changes to ruggedness.

In a mile and a half, a harrowing tale awaits you at Boise Rock. Although this site right off the parkway requires more imagination than what the rock itself offers, take a look. Seeing the actual place of Thomas Boise's ordeal puts the fierce experience into perspective.

Weather can brew and bubble up terrifying storms in these mountains. So when Boise set out with his horse in deep winter through the notch, he rode into the tight funnel of gushing wind, cold, and snow with impunity. The snowstorm quickly developed into a blizzard, and Boise got caught in it. What was he to do?

By fortune, he came upon this tilting, overhanging boulder (actually, it's called a glacial erratic—an isolated boulder left over from the retreating glaciers). He killed and skinned his horse, wrapped himself in the skin, and cowered under the rock. In the morning after the blizzard had subsided, rescuers found Boise encased in the frozen skin. They hacked him free with axes. He was still alive.

To the right of the Boise Rock parking lot, a large iron kettle catches running spring water from a spout. This Paul Bunyan-size kettle is all that remains of the early nineteenth-century New Hampshire Iron Factory Company, known locally as the Franconia Iron Works. Ore Hill, near Sugar Hill outside the notch, supplied the ore that the factory smelted into stoves, shovels, crowbars, chains, and soup kettles.

Old Man of the Mountain

Ranking as *the* symbol of New Hampshire, this startlingly impressive natural rock formation reigns among the peaks of the White Mountains—but only at strategic viewing points. Traveling north on the parkway, you'll find two viewing locations. Visit them both.

From Boise Rock, the first turnoff for the Old Man of the Mountain is only three-quarters of a mile up the road. At this spot, you'll be looking up and over the parkway at a cliff-edge legacy from 25,000 years ago. The jut-jawed face, with its aquiline nose and sturdy brow almost defying whatever the future has in store, consists of five separate ledges, 40 feet from chin to forehead. The face overlooks the notch from 1,200 feet above the parkway. With the graceful silhouette of the mountain below, the Old Man of the Mountain strikes a commanding, awe-inspiring pose.

Its human history began, not with the Abenakis or other Native Americans, who left no legends about it, but with Luke Brooks and Francis Whitcomb, who discovered the Old Man in 1805. Word spread, and so did its association with the flinty men and women of New Hampshire.

In short order, Daniel Webster had this to say about the old man: "Men hang out their signs indicative of their respective trades: shoemakers hang out a gigantic shoe; jewelers, a monster watch; and the dentist hangs out a gold tooth; but up in the mountains of New Hampshire, God Almighty has hung out a sign to show that there He makes men."

In 1850, Nathaniel Hawthorne wrote his short story "The Great Stone Face," titled after the Old Man's nickname. This story spread the fame of the formation around the country and in the early part of the twentieth century helped save the White Mountains from irreversible commercialization.

Today Niels Nelson, Jr., and his family maintain the structural integrity of the Old Man, as they have been doing since 1965. Three times a year, they climb to the Old Man to inspect and repair whatever damage frost, weeds, and wind have inflicted. Niels's son Dave will take over top billing when his father can no longer step across one particular six-foot gap between two stones on the Old Man. He calls this gap "Decision Rock."

The second view of the Old Man of the Mountain awaits less than one-half mile north on the other side of the parkway. Definitely spend some time at this spot, too. It's a pleasant walk of about 1,800 feet to the viewing location. Some information stations along the way fill in what you don't see, such as the needle pinnacle where eagles sometimes nest, a birch's roots growing around a troublesome boulder, or the hundred species of birds flying in the area and over Profile Lake directly before you at the base of the Old Man.

Most of all, you'll learn how Franconia Notch has attracted tourists since the mid-1800s. In the 1860s, the White Mountains drew tourists like a lodestone, and the Profile House resort in the shadow of the Old Man was enlarged annex by annex to accommodate the rush for recreation. By 1879, a railroad chugged to the doorstep of the resort. At one time, the resort stabled 350 horses. By 1905, the Profile House bragged about its newest addition, which sported 400 rooms and a lobby 250 feet long seating 500 people. And this was only one of the many hotels in operation during the era of the "Grand Hotels" in the Whites. At the Profile House alone, guests could choose among seventy items for lunch, including extensive varieties of meat, fish, fowl, wine, champagne, brandy, and French desserts.

By 1920, the automobile had replaced the train as the transportation of choice. Then in 1923, the Profile House burned down. To recoup the cost of lost tourist trade, lumber operators were called in to sweep away the trees for money, but a campaign to save the area from wholesale commercialization took root, seeded principally by the Society for the Protection of New Hampshire Forests, or the Forest Society. The state legislature agreed, after long negotiations, to spring for $200,000 to buy 6,000 acres in the notch if matching private funds could be raised for the project. In a triumphant national campaign appealing to all those who had enjoyed and prized Franconia Notch, the Forest Society matched that figure. More than 15,000 people contributed nationwide. That's the reason Franconia Notch, with all its wonders, still exists for us today.

Before getting back on the parkway, you may want to visit the Ski Museum. Turn left from the Profile Lake parking lot, where the Cannon Mountain ski slopes rise above. These slopes, with Echo Lake below, became the first engineered ski slopes more than fifty years ago and remain popular today. In summer, a seven-minute tram ride takes you up the mountain, overlooking four states and Canada at the peak.

Robert Frost Place

Get back on the Franconia Notch State Parkway and drive north onto the continuation of I-93. About six miles along, take exit 38, the second turnoff to Franconia village. Once you're off the interstate, turn left under the bridge. You'll see the sign for the Robert Frost Museum, which directs you straight through town.

Pass Elmwood Cemetery on the left, following this riverside road to the right. In one-half mile or so, two signs on the right—Bickford Hill Road and Frost Place—direct your next turn. Follow the signs, and you're there in a minute.

From a small, inconspicuous parking lot, walk a very short way up the unpaved road to the mailbox with "R. Frost" painted on the side. The low-standing, unassuming white house overlooks the Kinsman Mountain Range, with Mount Lafayette and pointed Mount Liberty regal across the sweeping valley.

Robert Frost lived in New Hampshire from his eleventh to his forty-fifth year, producing most of his cherished poems while in this state. He lived year-round in his Franconia farmhouse from 1915 to 1921, then stayed there for seventeen summers thereafter.

Today the house, now listed on the National Register of Historic Places, stands in honored testimony to the power of ideas and art. A visit to the Frost Place offers an opportunity to pay homage to the poet, who continues to give us pleasure and beauty.

Most likely your introduction to the relaxed tour will be the video produced by Frost's grandson Ben and shown in the barn out back. Since 1977, working poets-in-residence have read their works during the summer, underscoring the vitality of the place.

The Poetry and Nature Trail in the adjoining forest combines Frost's poems, on plaques, with appropriate woodland scenes. "Evening in a Sugar Orchard" and "Goodby and Keep Cold" are displayed in the woods where he wrote them. "Stopping by Woods on a Snowy Evening," "Mending Wall," and other poems also appear along the half-mile trail.

Refreshed and exhilarated, drive farther down the Frost Place road about three-quarters of a mile to the end. Follow the sign on the left to Route 116, which you'll meet in a minute or two.

As a wrap-up of the area, turn right onto Route 116. The circle to Franconia village takes you by fine country inns. In less than one-half mile, the Franconia Inn, with the White Mountains as a backdrop, is worth a look, and maybe even a stop. The town airport operates directly across the road. At the end of the airstrip, turn left onto Wells Road and take a drive through the woods. The Horse and Hound Inn, one and a half miles along, invites another look. One-half mile farther on, Wells Road intersects Route 18. Turn left, and in two-tenths of a mile, you'll see Lovett's Inn, which has a good reputation for country dining and accommodations.

In another mile or so, you'll be back in Franconia.

In the Area

All phone numbers are within area code 603.

Cannon Mountain, Franconia: 823-5563

Franconia Inn: 823-5542 or 800-473-5299

This mailbox marks the location of Robert Frost's home in Franconia.

Franconia Notch State Park: 823-5563

Frost Place, Franconia: 823-5510

Horse and Hound Inn, Franconia: 823-5501

Lovett's Inn, Franconia: 823-7761 or 800-356-3802

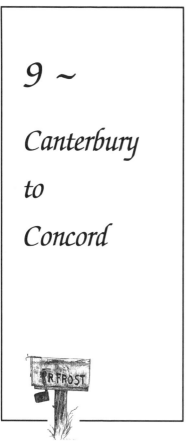

9 ~

Canterbury

to

Concord

From Nashua, Manchester, and Concord: Take I-93 north to exit 18, then follow the signs to the Canterbury Shaker Village. From Hanover and Lebanon take I-89 south to Concord, then I-93 north to exit 18 east. This trip runs approximately 41 miles.

Highlights: *The Canterbury Shaker Village, the Gilmantons, Turtle Pond, Forest Society headquarters.*

Canterbury Shaker Village

The seven-mile drive from exit 18 on I-93 north above Concord introduces you to Canterbury Shaker Village. A country road winding through the woods slows the world and soothes the spirit, just what the Shaker legacy prescribes.

One-half mile from the highway, a small open field and farmhouse presage what's to come. Immediately, veer right at the junction (a sign to the Shaker Village directs the way), then steer up a short hill and onto high land and more compact fields. In a minute or so, turn right onto Route 132 south, then quickly left at the next junction. (Efficient Shakers have posted another sign for you.)

After another mile, you'll clear the top of a hill, and Canterbury Center will appear before you. You'll find plenty

Canterbury United Community Church

of room to park and look around. Give way to the irresistible sightseeing impulse. This (non-Shaker) village captures much of the visual simplicity of yesteryear and the self-sufficiency found in essential buildings surrounding a town center. Everything's here: the 1736 Canterbury Town Hall for government, the Canterbury United Community Church for the spirit, the Canterbury Country Store for the body, the Elkins Public Library for the mind, the town gazebo for celebration, and the town cemetery for memories.

Go straight up the hill past the Canterbury Elementary School on the right. The next four miles or so undulate through the countryside. Look for the Peverly Meadows Conservation Area, a wetlands, on the left. A turnout allows you to watch for beavers and their dam a short distance from the road, although chances are that the shy animals will stay out of sight. In about one-half mile, proceed straight ahead through a crossroads with a compact 1796 house on the corner.

At a stop sign coming up shortly, veer to the left, as instructed. Soon the extensive sloping fields of the Shaker Village parallel the road on the right. Canterbury Shaker Village encompasses a hilltop complex of twenty-three buildings, fenced in white and situated at appealing angles and in attractive groupings. A main meetinghouse at the funnel end of a mighty row of maples welcomes visitors with an extraordinary combination of stateliness and simplicity in the Shaker tradition.

Touring the grounds takes you inside some of the white clapboard buildings. You'll see the practicality of these people: pegs on the walls for getting unused chairs out of the way, simple furniture for easy use and cleaning, uncluttered floors and rooms to sharpen the spirit.

This particular village became the sixth of eventually nineteen Shaker villages in this country. Founded in the 1780s, Canterbury Shaker Village bloomed into a thriving community, reaching its peak in 1860, when more than 300 men and women lived and worked the 4,000-acre complex. At one point, 100 buildings of varying sizes and uses stood on the grounds.

The hour-and-a-half tour teaches you about the thoughts, impulses, and human spirit that supported the building of this amazing village. Equality formed the basis for much of what founder Ann Lee (1736–1784) believed when she emigrated from England to the New World. This stemmed from her belief in both the existence and the equality of the feminine aspect of God—God the Father/Mother. In practical terms, this meant that her communities relied on equal work and input by men and women.

In fact, the Shakers, first organized in 1776, put to the test the Declaration of Independence, also issued in 1776, which stated that all men were equal. Whereas Shaker women could participate in the political governance of their communities, women of the new Republic had no legal voting rights until 1920. Here's what the Shakers held to be true, quoted from an early statement of belief:

Equality of the Sexes, in all departments of life.
Equality of Labor: all working for each, and each for all.
Equality in Property,—No rich, no poor. Industrial
    freedom. Consecrated labor. Dedicated wealth. A
    united Inheritance.
Each using according to need.
Each enjoying according to capacity.
Freedom of Speech. Toleration of Thought and Reli-
    gion. Often persecuted, Shakers have never been
    known to persecute.
Abolition of all Slavery.—Chattel. Wage. Habit. Pas-
    sion. Poverty. Disease.
Temperance in all things.
Justice and Kindness to all living beings.

Practical Benevolence. Thou shalt love thy neighbor as thyself.
True Democracy. Real Fraternity. Practical Living of the Golden Rule.

Ann Lee emphasized the practical and the ideal, with daily manual labor for all under the maxim "Hands to work and hearts to God." As for leaders, both sexes played major roles in both spiritual and temporal matters. The last of the living Shakers at Canterbury, Sister Ethel Hudson, died in September, 1992. The village now operates under a benevolent trust to maintain public education about Shakerism and to keep up the beauty of the buildings and grounds. Although individual Shakers no longer live here to carry on the traditions, the village is a testament to the Shakers' important contribution to American life.

The Gilmantons

The Shaker Village is the highlight of this route, but the rest of the semicircular trip also holds some pleasant surprises.

From the Shaker Village parking lot behind the red-brick office, turn left and continue north toward Belmont, about six miles away. This narrow backcountry road takes you early on past Hills Corner Farm, with horses on a hilltop, and some dense woods.

At a junction nearly two and a half miles along, veer to the right, then continue straight ahead. Go past Old Gilmanton Road a little over a mile later. Increasingly more houses appear as you approach Belmont. At the stop sign stop right before the town center, pick up Route 140 east (straight ahead), then turn left on Route 140 in a very short distance. Proceed past the junction of Route 106, heading uphill on Route 140 toward Gilmanton.

Four miles of easy driving takes you to Gilmanton, with its early nineteenth-century charm. At the junction of Route 107, detour both left and right on 107 for a short cruise by some houses that typify New Hampshire longevity.

Return to Route 140 east and continue on toward Gilmanton Iron Works, nearly seven miles away. More casual driving is in store, with some farm fields and soft hills along the way. As the town name suggests, this area supplied iron ore for early mining and smelting operations.

Once you drive downhill to the center of Gilmanton Iron Works, turn right at the Village Store onto Stage Road. This leads you deep into the country, past a family-operated sawmill and a few isolated small farms. Turn left at the stop sign, and in short order you'll be in the small village of Lower Gilmanton. Take Route 129 west to Loudon and Concord. In one-half mile, you'll be glad you did. An open, peaceful pond gives you a good opportunity to stop and stretch.

In another two and a half miles, go straight through a crossroads at Loudon Center. Up ahead, Meadow Ledge Farm invites you to pick your own apples in early fall. Maple syrup and farm-fresh vegetables also are available.

In less than ten minutes, the light at the junction of Route 106 signals you to be alert for Oak Hill Road, which will take you to East Concord.

Loudon and the Forest Society

At the junction of Routes 106 and 129, proceed across Route 106 into Loudon. In a short distance, turn right at the Maxfield Public Library onto School Street. One-half mile later, turn left onto Oak Hill Road, and you're home free.

Oak Hill Road passes pretty rural land and homes. In a couple of miles, a lift in the terrain overlooks a long-view clearing. Another mile and a half down the road is silky Turtle Pond, with plenty of wide-open shoreline to enjoy.

The Turtle Pond boat access comes up fast on the right (a sign points the way). Drive onto the paved access to get a good sense of the Turtle Pond Conservation Area and twenty-three acres of wetlands surrounding you.

Less than two miles farther along, the homes in East Concord crowd closer together. Proceed downhill to a stop sign at Mountain Road, where I-93 is visible. Look to the far left, where the "Conservation Center" sign directs you back uphill on Eastside Drive. In three-quarters of a mile, follow Portsmouth Street to the Forest Society headquarters. You can't miss it.

The official name of the Forest Society is the Society for the Protection of New Hampshire Forests. This kingpin organization, highly respected for its sensible, long-term environmental achievements in the state, works with business, industry, environmentalists, and nature lovers to develop and maintain some of the exotic and simple sites along the country roads you've traveled.

The solar-heated headquarters in sheltering pines has a small gift shop and an impressive skyline view of Concord across the Merrimack River. If you have questions about the abundance of natural wonders in New Hampshire, the answers await you here.

In the Area

Both phone numbers are within area code 603.

Canterbury Shaker Village: 783-9511

Society for the Protection of New Hampshire Forests, Concord: 224-9945

10 ~

Grand
Monadnock

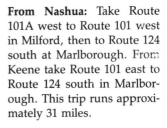

From Nashua: Take Route 101A west to Route 101 west in Milford, then to Route 124 south at Marlborough. From Keene take Route 101 east to Route 124 south in Marlborough. This trip runs approximately 31 miles.

Highlights: *Grand Monadnock, The Inn at East Hill Farm, Fitzwilliam, antiques stores, Franklin Pierce College, Cathedral of the Pines, Jaffrey Center, the Monadnock Inn.*

Marlborough

The starting point for this tour is the junction of Routes 101 and 124 on the east side of Marlborough. Before turning onto Route 124, take a look inside the Homestead Bookshop, just beyond the junction on Route 101. This friendly, chock-full store is set slightly back on the right. You'll find a wide spectrum of old books—just about all the fiction and non-fiction titles you've always wanted to read, including lots of New Hampshire-related books (at proper country road prices).

Go back to Route 124 and immediately begin a steady climb. On the left is the Frost Free Library, which sports a granite-block façade with a big sign (no doubt one of the most photographed signs in the universe). In deep winter, when the library is encrusted with snow and ice, the Frost Free Library becomes known far beyond the Marlborough town limits.

Grand Monadnock

In four-tenths of a mile, Route 124 curves over a gentle hill, and fabled Grand Monadnock juts up before you. Here is a sweeping, open view of the mountain. Many more such views await you along this route.

After two more miles of tree-lined driving past an antiques store and a stately red-brick nineteenth-century house, look for a narrow opening on the left. The street sign for Monadnock Drive stands a few yards off Route 124. A cleared field gives you a close-up view of the mountain, its symmetrical west side fully visible.

In another 1.7 miles, an engrossing scene breaches the woods at Perkins Pond. Route 124 quickly slants down into a marsh clearing on both sides of the two-lane road. Park in the small turnout and linger over this breathtaking sight. The mountain, rocky and bald at the summit, rises behind a wedge of wetlands rimmed with water lilies in summer, aflame with color in autumn, icy and hibernating in winter, and Irish green in spring.

The story of Grand Monadnock could fill a book. Its appeal encompasses far more than geological features; the social and literary history related to the mountain equals these attractions. Surprisingly, the peak reaches a modest 3,165 feet—barely a pimple on the planet compared to the towers of the Rockies, Sierra Nevada, Alaska Range, Andes, and Himalayas.

The singular location of this peak makes it stand out. Rising 2,000 feet above the surrounding plain, the mountain became the prototype for the technical geological term *monadnock*, a summit that stands alone. The Native Americans called it "the place of the unexcelled mountain." On a clear day, you can see all six New England states from the summit. Boston's skyscrapers are visible on the horizon. In fact, nineteenth-century climbers looked through telescopes for friends and relatives on tall ships sailing into Boston Harbor.

In the early 1800s, a man-made fire to rid the mountain of a wolf preying on sheep burned off summit trees and brush, leaving the peak permanently bald. Thousands of hikers every year climb the five main trails to this rocky top.

In the second half of the 1800s, taverns and resorts around Grand Monadnock catered to the city folk who vacationed here. Henry David Thoreau camped on Grand Monadnock three times and wrote of his experiences. Ralph Waldo Emerson wrote poems of "the airy citadel." Nathaniel Hawthorne: "Monadnock was visible like a sapphire against the sky." Rudyard Kipling: "Monadnock came to mean everything that was helpful, healing, and full of quiet." Mark Twain: "In these October days Monadnock and the valley and its framing hills make an inspiring picture." John Greenleaf Whittier, Oliver Wendell Holmes, William Ellery Channing, Willa Cather (buried in nearby Jaffrey Center), Abbott Thayer, William Phelps, George de Forest Brush, Augustus St. Gaudens, and many other writers, poets, and artists recorded the impact of Grand Monadnock on them.

Today Grand Monadnock remains enchanting, because beginning in 1883 increasing numbers of people rallied to save the summit from commercialization. Thanks to the efforts of far-sighted individuals and the energetic leadership of the Society for the Protection of New Hampshire Forests over the years, the mountain now enjoys environmental honor as Monadnock State Park. Today no cash registers, radio towers, ski lifts, roads, or eateries sully this magnificent peak.

Hikers must earn their Monadnock. The shortest trail of 1.9 miles, the White Dot Trail beginning at park headquarters, requires some rock-ledge climbing and heavy breathing. If you don't want to make the climb, you can still appreciate the mountain's beauty from afar.

Fitzwilliam

Before continuing on to Fitzwilliam, turn right at the sign for the Inn at East Hill Farm (one-tenth of a mile on Route 124 from Perkins Pond, at the base of Grand Monadnock). A short way up the hill, another sign announces the inn.

The working farm of 150 acres combines the tending of sheep, goats, cows, and chickens with the care of vacationers. This rural family resort offers a swimming pool overlooking Grand Monadnock, hayrides and hikes in summer, sleigh rides and cross-country skiing in winter, and many other activities. It's the kind of place that assures you that vacations without glitz and forced fun still exist.

For now, backtrack down the hill and turn onto Route 124. In a mile and a quarter, a sign for the Old Toll Road Trail appears on the left. In Thoreau's day, horses and buggies took visitors up this mile-long road to the Half Way House resort. The hotel burned in 1954, and the unpaved road is no longer open to motor vehicles. But if you're so inclined, park your car at the trailhead and walk the easy mile to the old resort site, which as the original name suggests lies halfway up the mountain. Views from this cleared, flat site stretch for miles. Trails to the summit start at this point. They require more effort than the Old Toll Road.

Continue down Route 124 for another half mile, where a large, open field with a classic stone wall reveals another view of Grand Monadnock. At the end of the field, a sign indicates an unnamed road on the right, opposite an old red farmhouse, which leads to Fitzwilliam. Consider this four-mile back byway a connecting road. In little less than a mile, veer right onto Old Fitzwilliam Road (at last a sign; you're on the right road). At this juncture, you'll see a fine old brick house on your right, with Grand Monadnock behind it. As you approach the end of this connector, more upcountry houses appear, along with a well-fashioned stone wall, a small pond, and some sheep.

At the junction of Route 12, proceed straight across to a very short connector, which leads to the 1796 Fitzwilliam Inn. The three-story inn was a skyscraper in its day. In 1893, telephones linked guests with Boston and beyond, just as they do today. No telephones ring in the guest rooms, however; modern conveniences intrude only so far.

Fitzwilliam played a midpoint role on the bumpy road from Boston to Hanover. In the early days, the inn benevolently interrupted the body-banging stagecoach ride with legendary relief. Ambiance permeates this welcoming inn, open to the public for meals.

Diagonally from the inn, the oblong town green, outlined by granite posts and wooden rails, invites a saunter around the common. The steepled town hall and the town library next door stand on one side, with the Fitzwilliam Community Church at the far end. The sign in front of the church states that it was first organized in 1774, and the building built in 1857, which may be confusing. During the early years of this country, a "church" was a gathering of people, a community of like-minded individuals and families. A "meetinghouse" was the building in which the "church" met. The meetinghouse was also the seat of town government, the place where school rules and laws were formulated, and the site of yearly, monthly, and sometimes weekly town meetings to decide local laws. The meetinghouse played a central part as the site of free speech and truly democratic government decision making—much as it does in most New Hampshire small towns today. The old rutted road from Hanover to Boston conveyed the New Hampshire Minutemen to battle in 1776. James Reed had settled in Fitzwilliam in 1765 as the original proprietor of Monadnock No. 4. (The early townships surrounding Grand Monadnock were named and numbered.) After the Battle of Lexington in 1775, he recruited men to form the Third New Hampshire Regiment, which supported General John Stark at the Battle of Bunker Hill. Reed was commissioned a brigadier general after his engagement at the Battle of Ticonderoga.

Fitzwilliam bulges with history. It has many antiques shops and other stores that offer good browsing.

Cathedral of the Pines

From the Fitzwilliam Inn, return downhill the short distance to the junction of Route 12. At the stop sign, go straight onto Route 119. The five miles to Franklin Pierce College cover benign woodlands, with an occasional house along the way. When the marsh on the right catches your eye, you'll soon pass Pearly Pond on the left, a calming sight.

After another bend in the road, the entrance to the college is on your left. The three-quarter-mile entrance road parallels Pearly Pond. At the stop sign at the top of the hill, turn left to the campus center, overlooking the pond. Steer around and up to the dormitory section for a brilliant view of Grand Monadnock.

Return to Route 119 and turn left. In little more than a mile, continue straight through the traffic signal at the junction of US 202 and Route 119. Follow 119 east up the grade and past the sign for Rindge Center on the right. In about one-half mile, turn left at the sign for the Cathedral of the Pines.

A mile and a half later, turn into the entrance to the Cathedral of the Pines. When Lieutenant Sanderson Sloane lost his life in an airplane crash during the Second World War, his parents established this memorial on the land where he had planned to build his home after the war. In 1957, the U.S. Congress voted to recognize this as a memorial to all American war dead. A striking bell tower at the entrance stands as the only monument in this country to women who have died in war. Four bronze bas-reliefs by Norman Rockwell adorn the sides of the tower.

The landmark displays an array of religious, fraternal, and sororal mementos and provides a place for services and patriotic gatherings. Exquisite stones and plaques donated from social organizations decorate the Hilltop House. The museum downstairs displays religious and military illustrations and artifacts. Pathways lead to meditation stations.

The Altar of the Nation is the primary draw at the Cathedral. At scheduled services, weddings, and memorials, participants and visitors walk down the outdoor aisle of benches and either stand or sit overlooking a most stupendous view. In the distance, a silhouette of Grand Monadnock cuts the long horizon, while peaceful woodlands fill the space between the Cathedral of the Pines and the great mountain.

Jaffrey Center

At the exit to the Cathedral of the Pines, turn left and drive a little less than a mile to the Annett State Forest. Look for its modest entrance sign on the right at the bottom of a hill. Drive slowly over this unpaved, narrow, bumpy road. (Don't do this in mud season.) The road eases through evergreen woods and arrives at a small reservoir dam. This little-known lake prompts you to get out of your car and look around. You can cross to the other side of the dam or follow the road along the lakeshore. Quiet and tranquil.

Return to the paved road, and in another two-tenths of a mile you'll come to the Annett Forest State Park wayside picnic area, a handy spot for a snack. In another half mile, veer left at a Y junction with a sign saying "Jaffrey—Home of Mt. Monadnock." Within a mile, the settlement of Squantom, with 1820s houses and a lumber mill, quickly fades into woods again.

Proceed straight through a crossroads for one-tenth of a mile, then turn left onto Contoocook Road, at the sign for the Woodbound Inn. A few minutes later, after a rejuvenating drive past Contoocook Lake and a small golf course, you'll see the Woodbound Inn.

Continue down this back road for a mile and a half to a stop sign. Turn right and go three-tenths of a mile to US 202. Pool Pond lies straight ahead. Take a right onto US 202.

Mount Monadnock viewed across Gilmore Pond

In 1.3 miles (right after a slight rise and soft curve in the road), look for Mountain View Road on the left. Take the quick left and right turns on Mountain View Road uphill three-tenths of a mile to the dead end. Expansive Gilmore Pond, with an island of trees and an in-and-out shoreline, spreads out before you. Grand Monadnock looms in the distance.

Return to US 202 and turn left. Continue one and a half miles to the heart of Jaffrey. At the blinking light—the junction of Routes 124 and 137—turn right onto Route 124 and continue through town and over the hill. Addison's, an appealing gift shop and quick food stop, will soon appear on the right. Backtrack on Route 124 and cruise up a slight grade through Jaffrey and out of town. In less than two miles, the road will slow you down for Jaffrey Center, a small village that still looks much the way it did in the early years. You can't miss the Monadnock Inn on your left, the only local inn that has continued to be open since the early twentieth-century resort era faded. This is a charming place for a tasty meal.

At the top of the hill, the old Jaffrey Center green has a long history, including the first church of Jaffrey, organized in 1780. The red one-room schoolhouse stands out against the bordering maples.

Just beyond the schoolhouse, the town cemetery lies shrouded by more maples and oaks. In the left-hand corner stands the headstone of Willa Cather, the Nebraska-born novelist who wrote *My Antonia* and *Death Comes to the Archbishop* while living in the shadow of Grand Monadnock. The stone reads, " . . . that is happiness, to be dissolved into something complete and great."

In the early years, Jaffrey Center manufactured 40 percent of all the tacks produced in the United States. In the mid-1800s, Aunt Hannah Davis made, trademarked, and sold this country's first wooden bandboxes. Amos Fortune, born a free man and son of a king in Africa, was sold as a slave in Massachusetts in 1725. At age sixty he purchased his freedom and settled in Jaffrey, where he established a tannery. When he died in 1801, one of the most respected citizens of Jaffrey, he left his estate to the Jaffrey church and school. Today his tombstone can be found in the village churchyard, commemorating a man "who was born free in Africa, a slave in America, who purchased his liberty, professed Christianity, lived reputably, and died hopefully." Elizabeth Yates's Newberry Award-winning book, *Amos Fortune, Free Man*, traces the history of this remarkable man.

From Jaffrey Center, continue downhill one-quarter mile. Turn right to visit the headquarters of Monadnock State Park two miles farther on. Or continue straight on Route 124 back to your starting point in Marlborough.

In the Area

All phone numbers are within area code 603.

Addison's, Jaffrey: 532-7062

Cathedral of the Pines, Rindge: 899-3300

Fitzwilliam Inn: 585-9000

Franklin Pierce College, Rindge: 899-4000 or 800-437-0048

Homestead Bookshop, Marlborough: 876-4213 or
800-834-3618

Inn at East Hill Farm, Troy: 242-6495 or 800-242-6495

Monadnock Inn, Jaffrey Center: 532-7001

Monadnock State Park, Jaffrey Center: 532-8862

Woodbound Inn, Jaffrey: 532-8341 or 800-688-7770

11 ~

Keene to East Westmoreland

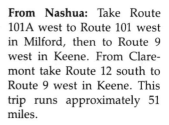

From Nashua: Take Route 101A west to Route 101 west in Milford, then to Route 9 west in Keene. From Claremont take Route 12 south to Route 9 west in Keene. This trip runs approximately 51 miles.

Highlights: *Chesterfield Gorge, Spofford Lake, Pisgah State Park, Road's End horse and ski touring farm, Hinsdale, Brattleboro, Vermont, backcountry.*

Chesterfield Gorge

In Keene, pick up Route 9 west at the junction of Routes 12 and 101. Keene, the largest city in the area (22,000 population), is nestled in a shallow valley rimmed with soft hills and old Grand Monadnock to the east.

To reach Chesterfield Gorge a little less than six miles away, drive on Route 9 west. In a couple of minutes, you'll begin a steady, gradual climb alongside scattered highway homes and small businesses. Three miles from Keene, you'll hit a steeper half-mile climb. Once you're over the top, proceed a little farther along until you see the sign for the Chesterfield Gorge State Wayside—A Geological Park on the right. The gorge cuts a short, narrow, rocky waterway through the woods. In the parking lot, you'll find a small visitors center with local artifacts and brochures, a picnic area, and rest rooms. Of course, the main attraction is the gorge.

To enjoy the gorge up close, follow its edge in a loop, which means some up-and-down walking. Sturdy footwear will keep your steps more secure over exposed tree roots and rock surfaces.

Plan a relaxed half hour for this pleasant saunter. Walk down the 300 yards from the parking lot to the determinedly placed log slanting to the right. At this point, you'll see a footbridge at the top of the chasm. Once you're on the other side (a very short distance), a well-worn path leads you down the edge of the gorge, in places fenced in for safety. The high woods, the thrash of water, the jumbled slabs of granite, the aroma of pine needles underfoot, and the chiseled strength of the gorge will hold your attention and refresh your spirit.

At the bottom of the gorge, another footbridge takes you across the water and rocks. Then up you climb on the other side for a different view of the same engrossing sight.

Spofford Lake

One-half mile along on Route 9, turn right onto Route 9A west to Spofford village, a simple, cloistered, bottom-of-the-hill town with a country store and volunteer fire department. Less than a minute later, as you drive uphill, take a right at the post office onto North Shore Road. One-quarter mile later, turn right at the junction and cruise through this rural residential area, with glimpses of Spofford Lake flashing through the trees on your left. Finally, a mile later at the top of a hill, a full view of the lake opens up.

The road encircles the lake, and as you continue driving, hints of more views to come sparkle between the cottages along the road. Less than a mile from the wide-open hilltop view, the town beach comes up fast on your left. Overall, the state owns a lake proper, while individuals can own the land around a lake for exclusive use. But some minimal access to a lake or pond must be available to the general public, either for a beach or a boat landing. "Minimal" is the key at Spofford Lake.

Keep on cruising to a stop sign on Route 63 about a mile later. Turn left, and in less than a minute, the road hugs the cottageless shoreline for a half-mile stretch. New Hampshire enjoys an extraordinary bounty of lakes and ponds, and this one shows the pacific side of flat water as effectively as Chesterfield Gorge shows its rugged side.

Chesterfield

When you reach the stop sign at Route 9, steer straight across onto Route 63 south to the village of Chesterfield, a mile up the bluff. The open common of Chesterfield is centered on three fine stone buildings—the town hall, public library, and post office. Across the street, a grassy expanse of the elementary school playground completes the rural village picture.

Behind the unornamented town center lie some appealing outreach roads. Take a look at two of them, both of which begin at Old Chesterfield Road next to the public library.

Drive past the elementary school for one-quarter mile until you reach the Pisgah State Park sign on the right. Turn onto Horseshoe Road and follow the macadam until the byway changes to a smooth, unpaved road. After easing through a tunnel of woods with scattered homes for a mile and a half, the road dead-ends into a parking area for the state park. Straight ahead, a clearing opens out on the distant waves of hills. To the right of the parking lot, a hiking trail slants into the wild. A posted box contains maps of the state park paths.

To the right is the birthplace of Chief Justice Harlan Fiske Stone. A rectangle of granite foundation stones marks the site. An upright block with a plaque states that "his fellow townsmen" erected the memorial in 1947. Justice Stone was born in 1872 at this site on Horseshoe Road. Eventually, Stone served as U.S. attorney general under President Calvin Coolidge, U.S. Supreme Court justice beginning in 1924, and chief justice of the court beginning in 1941, five years before his death.

Backtrack on Horseshoe Road to the stop sign where you first turned toward the park. Turn right and continue down Old Chesterfield Road toward Road's End Farm, a horsemanship camp and ski touring center. After passing the Ware-Joslyn Cemetery (1851) on the right, in one-half mile veer right at the Y junction (you'll see a Road's End sign).

Road's End Farm lies, naturally, at the end of the road, less than a mile away now. This road, tucked away in hidden repose, passes a mixture of ancient maples, husky oaks, undulating fields, stone walls, and brook-creased gullies. If you're lucky, a dozen or more horses will be out in the field as you approach the farm. On your left, a pond at the bottom of a steep hill might be surrounded by Canada geese in autumn. A colossal blue barn overlooks the rest of the cleared field stretching from the geese pond to a sumptuous hill for horseback riding in summer and cross-country skiing in winter. This dual-season farm caters to horse and ski lovers with appropriate trails across the rivers and into the woods. Neighboring Pisgah State Park is a buffer against city bustle. At certain outlooks on the high hills, Spofford Lake to the north patches the horizon with seasonal blue or white.

Return to Chesterfield village and turn left onto Route 63 south.

Hinsdale and Brattleboro, Vermont

As you drive from Chesterfield to Stage Road (about one-half mile), glance to the right between the houses and over the fields. There, in the distance, the Green Mountains of Vermont ripple their way north on the other side of the Connecticut River. For more than half the seven and a half miles to Hinsdale, the road slants down the terrain, a wooded country drive as you skirt the western edge of Pisgah State Park.

Soon you're in the rural outskirts of Hinsdale. At the first stop sign since Chesterfield (the junction of Route 119 in downtown Hinsdale), look straight across the street at two grand Victorian buildings, their turrets and balconies reminiscent of a bygone era. Turn right onto Main Street and steer straight down past an abandoned mill on the left. Then follow Route 119 uphill.

A mile or so outside of town, the Connecticut River suddenly appears around a bend. This meandering river, its islands and sandbars splitting the casual flow, drains the hills you've been driving through. A sometimes shy river, the Connecticut is barely visible through the crowded summer woods. Leafless winter makes the river bolder.

The road, now heading north, moves inland slightly. In a couple of miles, you'll pass Hinsdale Greyhound Park (for dog racing) on the right. Continue another three miles, and Route 119 will take you over the Connecticut River, an opportune time to see the beneficent river from midstream. Fortunately, the bridges are low and open for good viewing up and down the shoreline.

The second bridge leads you directly into Brattleboro, Vermont, a vibrant, old-time town. Turn right into town. If the shops don't tempt you, proceed uphill and straight on through the center. At the end of Main Street, veer to the right at a Y junction, cross over a tributary to the Connecticut River three-quarters of a mile later, and make do through a mile and a half of strip malls.

At the junction on I-93, turn right onto Route 9 east toward Keene. Cross an open, steel-trussed bridge over the Connecticut River and head back into New Hampshire.

Two miles into New Hampshire, you'll see the Chesterfield Inn on the left. Country elegance permeates the 1787 inn, which overlooks the Connecticut River valley and offers more comfort than Chesterfield residents ever dreamed possible in 1787. Enter the candle-lit dining room through the kitchen, where the chef prepares fine cuisine.

Less than four more miles on Route 9 east brings you to "decision corner." Continue straight on Route 9 east to return directly to Keene, or return by way of cordial backcountry driving through Westmoreland and East Westmoreland.

If you decide to do the latter, turn left onto Route 63 north. This takes you back along Spofford Lake. Continue on for a bit more than three and a half miles past snug woodlands

A large, well-kept barn in Westmoreland

until a field banks up against the road and you see Millbrook Sugar House on the right. Stop here to buy maple syrup and pumpkins in season.

Pass by Spofford Road a short distance along on the right and proceed to Westmoreland, a cozy town center. Turn right in the heart of town toward East Westmoreland. The road for the next four miles is winding and narrow. A wonderful barn and farm field crop up midway along the route, a trace of the hardscrabble life that tested the mettle of early settlers.

Turn right onto Route 12 south, a primary state highway, and drive toward Keene. In less than a mile, as you move uphill, you'll see the Summit Gift Barn on the right. Stop in to browse its extensive offerings.

Three miles later, the trees part and Grand Monadnock rules the horizon. This wonderful peak captures the skyline a couple more times as you approach your starting point in Keene.

In the Area

All phone numbers are within area code 603.

Chesterfield Inn, West Chesterfield: 256-3211 or
    800-365-5515

Road's End Farm, Chesterfield: 363-4703

Summit Gift Barn, Westmoreland: 352-3321

12 ~

Peterborough

to

Dublin

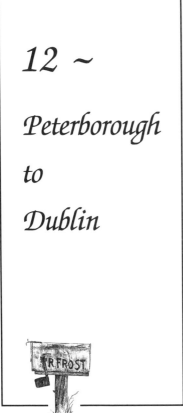

From Nashua: Take Route 101A west to Route 101 west in Milford, then to Miller State Park east of Peterborough. From Keene take Route 101 east to Miller State Park east of Peterborough. This trip runs approximately 43 miles.

Highlights: *Peterborough, Sharon Arts Center, Peterborough Players, Monadnock Summer Lyceum, Greenfield State Park, Zephyr Lake, antiques shops, Inn at Crotched Mountain, Tory Pines golf course, John Hancock Inn, Harrisville Designs, Howe Reservoir, Friendly Farm,* Yankee *magazine.*

Peterborough

A mountaintop overlook starts this trip out right. On Route 101, four miles east of Peterborough, drive up the 1.3-mile paved road to the summit of Pack Monadnock at Miller State Park.

The peak covers little more than a village green, but the view seems to cover the world—a wonderful spot for seeing the countryside you're about to drive through. Three sides of the summit open onto vast spreads of woodlands and mountaintops, including a spectacular shot of Grand Monadnock to the west. Picnic tables situated strategically provide a perfect spot to linger and lunch.

Note the fieldstone shelter built by the Civilian Conservation Corps (CCC) between 1933 and 1942, as well as markings for the Wapack Trail, a 21-mile pathway from Ashburnham, Massachusetts, to Greenfield, New Hampshire, the second town on this route.

Go down the summit road to the base parking lot, where at the edge of the woods, a flat-sided boulder is engraved with these words: "A. Erland & Hazil N. Goyette of Peterborough gave to the state of New Hampshire 421 acres of this mountain with its road and trails for the perpetual enjoyment of the public. September 1986."

Turn right onto Route 101, and in half a minute, omnipresent Grand Monadnock will spring forth on the horizon. About two and a half miles later, you'll come to Route 123 and Tewksbury's inviting gift shop. Turn left onto Route 123 and continue four miles to the Sharon Arts Center, a small, impressive gallery and high-quality gift shop. If you stay on Route 101, you'll come to the Black Swan Collection of Gifts on the left, another rewarding stop.

At the bottom of the hill, stop in at the Peterborough Chamber of Commerce, in the red building on the right, for answers about the Monadnock region. Then, turn right at the traffic signal for the half-mile trip along Grove Street to the heart of Peterborough.

An accomplished town of 5,000, Peterborough reputedly was the basis for Thornton Wilder's play *Our Town*, which was staged with the playwright in attendance at the Peterborough Players, a summer theater that has been operating for more than fifty years.

Wilder worked on the play in 1937 at the MacDowell Colony, up the hill to the left of the intersection of Grove and Main streets. As the first formally established artists' retreat, the colony originated in the early 1900s, when Marian Mac-

Dowell, wife of the celebrated composer Edward MacDowell, delivered lunch in a basket to her husband at an isolated log cabin where he worked undisturbed. When he died, energetic Marian traveled nationwide to generate support for developing the couple's more than 400 acres in the Peterborough woods as a secluded retreat. The colony offers writers and composers time and space for highly concentrated creative work in unseen, unvisited, untelephoned cottages. As always, the colonists meet only for breakfast and dinner; lunches in baskets are delivered at noon on cottage doorsteps. Thousands of colonists over the decades have worked on an extraordinary number of novels, compositions, paintings, and poems. Some well-known colonists have include E.A. Robinson, Leonard Bernstein, Willa Cather, and Elinor Wylie.

On Main Street, the 1826 Unitarian Church organizes and hosts the Monadnock Summer Lyceum, started by minister Abiel Abbott as the first lyceum in New Hampshire. Lyceum lectures and audience exchanges became a popular way of discussing key issues of the day. Ralph Waldo Emerson, Henry David Thoreau, Oliver Wendell Holmes, and Wendell Phillips spoke at lyceums in their day, but the movement diminished toward the end of the nineteenth century. In 1969, Unitarian minister David VanStrien of Peterborough revived the local series, and since then luminaries such as John Kenneth Galbraith, Sissela Bok, B.F. Skinner, Paul Tsongas, and Lester Thurow have spoken at the lyceum for the standard $100 fee and the honor of carrying on the American tradition of free speech.

Historical controversy over the origin of the town name leans toward Charles Mordaunt, Earl of Peterborough (Great Britain), not Peter Prescott, a secretary to one of the first New World proprietors. In 1738, the surveyor's report tells what kind of land early settlers were dealing with: "It began at a Black Burch Tree, ye South East Corner, and thence it Ran

West Six Miles and Sixty Eight Rods by a line of marked trees to a Spruce tree marked for ye South West corner. . . ."

The town was incorporated in 1760, and a little more than thirty years later, Peterborough became one of the first towns to establish a general library. The Peterborough Social Library heralded its lofty promise "to excite a fondness for books, to afford the most rational and profitable amusement, to prevent idleness and immorality, and to promote the diffusion of useful knowledge, piety, and virtue." In 1833, the Peterborough Town Library, under the impetus of Abiel Abbott, became the first free, tax-supported public library in the country. You'll find the same library a block down Main Street at the intersection of US 202, across the Contoocook River bridge.

To this day, Peterborough maintains a sense of cultural innovation. Writers and artists still gravitate to the town and surrounding area. Nationally known folk singers entertain at The Folkway restaurant, and the homegrown, stalwart Toadstool Book Shop reflects the tenor of its supportive, community-conscious clients. The Monadnock Music chamber orchestra performs its summer series here and in surrounding villages, and the New England Marionettes stages operas in the European puppet tradition.

Greenfield

Greenfield is an effortless five-and-a-half-mile drive away. In Peterborough, at the junction of Main Street and US 202, turn left onto 202. Follow US 202 1.6 miles to Route 136 east, where an open view of the Contoocook River spills over a dam to your left. Turn right onto Route 136.

At this point, a one-mile detour might interest you. Instead of turning onto Route 136, drive straight on US 202 to the headquarters and public showrooms of Brookstone (specialty tools) and Eastern Mountain Sports (outdoor clothing and equipment).

Otherwise, proceed to Greenfield on Route 136, a mostly flat road past a cows-and-geese farm, through rural residential areas, and by a small horse farm and backwater pond. One-half mile after you see a sign for Greenfield State Park (with a lakeside beach and nice camping and picnicking areas), you'll enter Greenfield center. The church meetinghouse is on the left, and the Bakery & Gift Shop/Denise's Restaurant is on the right. Set on a knoll, the church remains the oldest original meetinghouse in New Hampshire serving both church and state. Built in 1765, the steepled white building rose as a community effort of 100 volunteers from Greenfield and the surrounding villages. Ever since, it has acted as the center of church, government, and neighborhood activity.

Take a slow ride up the hill for a look at the upbeat houses, including the Greenfield Inn, a bed and breakfast stopover. Continue for about three or four minutes out Route 31 to Zephyr Lake, a charming pond with an impressive commercial history. In 1874, the first railroad chugged into Greenfield, linking the outback of New Hampshire to Boston. When the something-out-of-nothing Yankee idea of selling ice excited the local populace, Zephyr Lake became useful and profitable in winter. By 1909, ice warehouses could store 20,000 tons of 15-inch-square blocks of ice. By 1939, more than 600 railroad cars were shipping ice each year to the Whiting Milk Plant in Charlestown, Massachusetts, outside Boston. When electric refrigeration proved more efficient than packing ice with sawdust, the phenomenal ice-cutting business died out. The winter of 1947 saw the last ice shipped from Zephyr Lake.

Francestown

To reach Francestown from the center of Greenfield, turn onto Route 136 at the northeast side of the church. You'll immediately curve around uphill past a slanting cemetery. The four miles to Francestown take you past a swamp on the left and then through thick woods, with an occasional house by the side of the road.

Before the Revolution, Governor John Wentworth named this town after his wife, Frances Deering Wentworth. Twenty years after Francestown was incorporated in 1772, soapstone was discovered and quarried. The stone was shipped down to Greenfield, where it was milled into bed warmers, stoves, sinks, and other products, The soapstone business, which raised Francestown's reputation far beyond its town limits, lasted a century.

The 1787 homestead of Levi Woodbury (1789–1851) still stands handsomely across from the 1801 church meeting-house. Woodbury sported quite a résumé—New Hampshire legislator, judge, and governor; U.S. senator; secretary of the Navy; secretary of the treasury; and U.S. Supreme Court justice.

By 1900, the population of Francestown had dwindled by more than half to 693, and by 1920, it was down to 385. Even the maple trees on Main Street died of old age.

Today Francestown is alive with the sound of children and country living. Antiques shops a short distance on Route 136 east toward New Boston represent a renewed spirit. As you continue our trip north from the church on Route 47/Main Street to Bennington, you'll enjoy the half mile of eighteenth- and nineteenth-century homes.

Bennington

Take Route 47 north in Francestown. In two and a half miles, a short side trip takes you halfway up Crotched Mountain. (Turn left at the sign for the mountain. The Maitre Jacq Restaurant is located on this corner.) A very short distance up the same road takes you to Thistledown Handcrafts, a fine shop with many appealing items attractively displayed.

One mile up the hill is the Inn at Crotched Mountain. One-half mile farther along the road flattens out at the parking lot for the reopened Crotched Mountain ski slopes.

Continuing on Route 47, you'll see a sign for the Tory Pines golf course and condominiums, one-half mile off the highway. In about ten minutes, you'll be in unadorned Bennington. Pause at the stop sign next to the elementary school to take a look around. Prior to 1842, the Bennington locale served the nearby town of Hancock as "Hancock Factory." The Contoocook River (you'll pass it shortly) drops seventy-five feet in less than a mile, a made-to-order site for dams and hydropower. Five dams were built for mills beginning in 1783. By 1810, one of the first cotton mills in New England operated here, as well as a cutlery factory, a wool fulling mill, a gunpowder mill, a tannery, and the manufacturing home of Robinson's hammock-chairs, which were shipped out on the Peterborough-Hillsboro Railroad.

Despite all this economic activity, no residents of Hancock Factory gained positions on the Hancock governing board at the 1842 town meeting. In protest, forty residents organized efforts to incorporate their own town, which they did the following year. Future U.S. president Franklin Pierce of Hillsboro led the petition for the new town, whose name— Bennington—he suggested.

Turn right at Bennington center, then continue straight on (don't turn at the Routes 47 and 31 sign), veering left two-tenths of a mile later. This takes you alongside a river cascade adjacent to Monadnock Paper Mill, an early nineteenth-century hydropower site.

At the stop sign, turn left onto US 202 and continue through a small enclave of houses in about half a mile. To the left, the Contoocook River flows over the Monadnock Power Station of 1923; take a short detour to see it up close.

Otherwise, proceed south along US 202. On the left is an open, restful, lakelike bulge in the river.

Hancock

In a very short distance, Route 137 leads you right three miles to the welcoming fountain on Main Street in Hancock. This town was named for John Hancock, who owned 1,870 acres of town land. The prominent Bostonian never visited the town, however. Early residents of Hancock, incorporated in 1779, were so vexed after years of unanswered requests for a Hancock gift to the town that they threatened to change the town's name to York.

The irresistible John Hancock Inn on Main Street, operating since 1789, remains the oldest continuously operated inn in the state. The inn offers "Food for the hungry, drink for the thirsty, rest for the weary," as it did in the old days when the four- and six-horse stagecoaches rumbled through town three days a week from Bellows Falls, Vermont, en route to Nashua and the train at Boston.

Walk the earthen paths past the stately Main Street houses, some of them still with their sturdy Federal and lacy Carpenter Gothic fences. The fences prevented driven cattle and sheep from stomping front yards on their way to pasture. The 1820 church with a Paul Revere bell, the graveyard where Revolutionary War heroes were laid to rest, the Hancock Market, Norway Pond, and the Grange-converted-to-post-office are all within strolling distance of the village green.

Harrisville

To get to Harrisville, turn left onto Route 137 at the Hancock village green, steer downhill, and in four-tenths of a mile turn right uphill. In three miles, a marsh opens up on the left, where you should be alert for an important upcoming turn. One-half mile later, immediately after topping a grade, turn right onto what can generously be called a tertiary byway. (This is Hancock Road, but you'll see the identification sign only at the end, in Harrisville.)

Keep steady ahead for four and a half woodsy miles to Harrisville. Along the way, you'll parallel a white-water brook for a time, cross over a small bridge, and curve in and out along a lakeshore.

At the stop sign, turn right and steer uphill to Harrisville, a Lilliputian mill town from a bygone era. Despite the usual trend toward demolition rather than upkeep, the Filtrine Manufacturing Company, the Elm Research Institute, Harrisville Designs (wool fabrics and weavings), and other businesses have maintained the vitality of the red-brick town.

In this compact village, a chain of six large and small ponds, draining ten square miles, funnels into a water chute of power. The first settlers arrived in 1774, but the town took solid shape between 1820 and 1870. Much of Harrisville revolved around sheep raised in the nearby hills and the manufacture of woolen cloth, a complicated process of scouring,

Picturesque Harrisville,
a tiny mill town

picking, carding, spinning, warping, weaving, fulling, washing, dyeing, napping, and shearing. Some processes could be done in households, but fulling and finishing required machinery powered by the water-driven turbines in town.

Chesham

Drive past Harrisville Pond on the right, then turn left at the Y junction (following the sign to Marlborough). Continue 2.7 miles to a stop sign, across from the old Chesham railroad station, now a converted art gallery. Turn left and follow the road through the shallow valley town.

Chesham relaxes out of the way in undisturbed quiet. Off the beaten track, the trip to Chesham offers ponds and brooks along the roads only the locals know the names of.

Continue past the new elementary school and out of town toward Route 101, which you'll intersect in about five minutes. Turn left on Route 101 east, a two-lane primary state highway. In about three-quarters of a mile, a rest area at Howe Reservoir is a convenient stop. Grand Monadnock, in round-shouldered profile, rises to the south.

Continue on Route 101 for 1.7 miles. On the right is the seven-acre Friendly Farm, inviting all to wander through the fields and barnyards and commune with the cows, horses, pigs, goats, chickens, geese, donkeys, turkeys, rabbits, and sheep. Great for kids.

Dublin

Continue east on Route 101. Dublin Lake soon shimmers along the road on the right. Grand Monadnock looms closer, once beckoning countless widely recognized and other less recognized visitors to Dublin, which was known for a time as the summer home of Bostonians.

The village center one-half mile later slants down the east side of the hill. You can't miss the red building on the left—the main offices of far-reaching *Yankee* magazine, the *Old Farmer's Almanac*, and other publications. The friendly office lobby displays all sorts of appealing books, magazines, and other products.

At 1,493 feet elevation, Dublin stands tall as the highest village in New England. The town received its charter from King George III in 1771. Henry Strongman, a Scotch-Irishman, laid claim as the first rooted settler in the area. When the time came to change the name from lackluster Monadnock No. 3, Strongman was honored by having the town named after his hometown—Dublin, Ireland.

Across from the *Yankee* office, Joseph Appleton, in the early nineteenth century, sold Medford Rum at 3 cents a glass with sugar, 2 cents without. Such good times ensued from such good prices that in 1874, the new Hotel Appleton House became known, before it burned in 1908, as The Laffingwell.

In the Area

All phone numbers are within area code 603.

Black Swan Collection of Gifts, Peterborough: 924-7906

Brookstone, Peterborough: 924-8485

Elm Research Institute, Harrisville: 827-3048

Eastern Mountain Sports, Peterborough: 924-7231

Filtrine Manufacturing Company, Harrisville: 827-3321

The Folkway, Peterborough: 924-7484

Friendly Farm, Dublin: 563-8444

Greenfield Inn: 547-6327

Greenfield State Park: 547-3497

John Hancock Inn, Hancock: 525-3318

Harrisville Designs: 827-3333

Inn at Crotched Mountain, Francestown: 588-6840

MacDowell Colony, Peterborough: 924-3886

Maitre Jacq Restaurant, Francestown: 588-6657

Monadnock Music, Peterborough: 924-7610

Monadnock Paper Mill, Bennington: 588-3311

New England Marionettes, Peterborough: 924-4333

Peterborough Chamber of Commerce: 924-7234

Peterborough Players: 924-7585

Peterborough Town Library: 924-6401

Sharon Arts Center: 924-7256

Tewksbury's Gift Shop, Peterborough: 924-3224

Thistledown Handcrafts, Francestown: 588-3192

Toadstool Book Shop, Peterborough: 924-3543

Yankee Publishing, Dublin: 563-8111

13 ~

Crawford Notch

From Rochester: Take Route 16 north to Route 16A two miles north of North Conway. From Concord take I-93 north to exit 32 east at Lincoln, then Route 112 east (Kancamagus Highway) to Conway, then Route 16 north to Route 16A north of North Conway. This trip runs approximately 58 miles.

Highlights: *White Mountain National Forest, Intervale, Jackson, Crawford Notch State Park, Willey House, Crawford House, Mount Washington Hotel, Cog Railway up Mount Washington.*

Intervale and Jackson

A spectacular introduction to this trip spreads out from a high overlook about two miles north of North Conway on US 302. You'll exclaim at a valley of flatland fields funneling into the distance, with Mount Washington and its bulky cohorts scraping the sky. Over the generations, this region has drawn millions of vacationers. Some of the early resort inns remain popular today.

On your right, take Route 16A for about two miles through Intervale, past low-key, year-round homes and a number of small inns—New England Inn, Riverside Inn B & B, and Forest Inn.

Soon after the Swiss Chalet Motel, veer right onto Thorn Hill Road. (Or you can continue a short distance and pick up Route 16 north to Jackson.) Thorn Hill Road satisfies your sense of adventure for three miles. Just anticipate that this byway over Thorn Hill begins as an unapologetic bumpy back road (not a road to drive during an ice storm). A mountain view appears in one-half mile, with a few farm scenes coming up later on.

Once you're on the downside of the hill, more quick views of the White Mountains will flash through the woods. Then come The Inn at Thorn Hill, the Inn at Jackson, and others before a stop sign, where you'll turn right to go through Jackson center.

Turn right at a Y junction onto Route 16B for an enjoyable loop through more hill-and-inn country—Wildcat Inn at the town center, Christmas Farm Inn up the hill. You'll drive into high mountain country, with pastures and working farms.

One and a half miles from Jackson center, Route 16B makes a sharp hairpin turn to the left; just follow the signs. Then for the next two miles, the drive softens into snugly contours and solitude.

At a stop sign, turn left. In one-half mile, after traveling alongside a river, you'll emerge from the woods to find the Eagle Mountain Resort. This large, venerable hotel overlooks its own golf course and an exhilarating mountainscape. In winter, this homey inn is close to the ski slopes; in summer, it offers easy access to warm-weather outdoor life. The dining room swings open its wooden doors for the public, too.

About a mile later along a river cascade, a stop sign and right turn at the Wentworth Resort return you to the heart of Jackson. Drive for a minute or two, then turn left onto Route 16 south, where you'll soon pass the red covered bridge built by Charles Broughton of Conway in 1876, one of the most photographed bridges around.

Willey House

For the next twenty miles or so to Willey House, you'll be driving into increasingly more preserved country. First, drive two miles down Route 16 past Heritage New Hampshire and Storyland exhibit parks. Then turn onto US 302 west in Glen. The restaurants and motels thin out until the Attitash ski area takes over, with its attendant ski huts and chalets along the road.

Long views of Crawford Notch ahead break through the highway vistas. About two and a half miles past Bartlett comes the White Mountain National Forest, with the Saco River alongside the road. The mountains grow bigger as you delve deeper into the notch.

You're in Crawford Notch State Park now, and by the time you reach Crawford Notch Campground, a sheer cliff towers above the riverbed. You'll see the Arethusa Falls trailhead one-half mile before Dry River Campground. Over 200 feet, the falls rank as the highest in New Hampshire, but seeing them requires a 1.3-mile, huff-and-puff hike.

In a few minutes, Willey House offers an irresistible stopping place to gawk at the rugged, humbling cliffs. Take a look at Willey Pond, a trout exhibition pool on the east side of the road at 1,340 feet elevation. If you're lucky, you'll see brook, square-tail, and speckled trout.

Prior to 1771, Crawford Notch was known only to Native Americans. Four years after Timothy Nash, a hunter, arrived here, the road/trail he built wound through the gorge floor. In 1790, Abel and Hannah Crawford, with their son Ethan Allen, settled in the notch, eventually establishing an inn, cutting trails over the barren mountaintops, and guiding visitors to the summit of Mount Washington.

When you crane your neck to look at the gorge walls, imagine the toil and trouble of hacking a railroad line through here in 1857. The line was carved through territory that rose 1,639 feet in elevation over the 30 miles from North Conway to Fabyan on the north side of the notch. In the heart of the notch, the rails rose an average of 116 feet per mile for nine miles. Frankenstein Trestle stands 80 feet high and 500 feet long, Willey Brook Bridge 100 feet high and 400 feet long.

The famous Crawford Path, once it reaches the top of Mount Clinton, follows the unobstructed ridges above the timberline for more than five miles, offering both spectacular views and sudden danger from the volatile weather of these brooding mountains. Cleared in 1819, the Crawford Path remains the oldest continuously walked mountain trail in the country.

At the site of the Willey House, the Samuel Willey family and two hired hands noticed in early 1826 that a landslide had washed away part of a nearby cliffside. As a precaution, they decided to build a protective cavelike shelter in case of an emergency. On August 28, the Saco River swelled to twenty feet above normal overnight. From what can be determined, a landslide directly above the Willey House crashed downward and split in two, leaving the house untouched. But the family and hired hands were buried alive, evidently trying to reach their emergency cave or climb high to escape the mad river. The house itself was later turned into an inn, which burned in 1898.

Crawford House

Along the two and a half miles to the top of Crawford Notch, remnants of the old cliffside railroad line are visible. After leaving the official boundaries of Crawford Notch State Park, you'll see Saco Lake on the right and the 1891 railroad depot on the left, now refurbished as an information station operated by the Appalachian Mountain Club (AMC).

Crawford House Resort stood here, too. Abel Crawford and his son Ethan Allen built the first Crawford House in 1828. Ethan Allen's brother Thomas sold it two years before a fire in 1854 destroyed it. A fire also destroyed its replacement in 1859. After Colonel Cyrus Eastman built a third Crawford House, the resort catered to thousands of wonder-seeking visitors, including Daniel Webster, Nathaniel Hawthorne, John Greenleaf Whittier, and presidents Pierce, Grant, Hayes, Garfield, and Harding. This resort, too, burned to the ground in 1977.

Mount Washington Hotel

Go down the gentle slope of US 302, and in less than ten minutes, the captivating Mount Washington Hotel shines at Bretton Woods, magnificent against the tremendous Presidential Range and Mount Washington.

Anticipating the triumphant close of the Second World War, the U.S. government hosted representatives of forty-four countries at the Mount Washington Hotel in 1944 for the Bretton Woods Economic Summit. The conference established the World Bank, set the gold standard at $35 an ounce, and decided on the American dollar as the core of international exchange. The system worked for a quarter of a century in stabilizing the economic systems of the industrialized world.

Take a look at the hotel up close. Drive in and walk up the knoll-top entrance. This elegant resort, which overlooks a gorgeous landscape, continues its nineteenth-century tradition of resort life. The long porch and chandeliered lobby evoke a more genteel time.

Cog Railway

Continue along US 302 north for three-quarters of a mile until you see the right turn for the Cog Railway. In about another six and a half miles on a steady upgrade, you'll arrive at the train station. If you're lucky, Mount Washington will be clear and bright, and one of the plodding engines will be spewing a column of smoke high on the mountainside.

The second-steepest and the first cog railroad of its kind in the world, the Mount Washington Cog Railway was built in 1869 at a cost of $139,500. The incline on the three-mile trip to the 6,293-foot peak averages one foot up for every four feet in length.

The "Jacob's Ladder" section of the trip climbs at a 37 percent grade. The engine tilts to keep the water level even in the boiler. Each trip consumes a ton of coal, which an engineer shovels into the red-hot boiler. The boiler produces steam to power the toothed cog gears, which turn the engine's wheels.

The three-hour round trip rewards you (sometimes) with a four-state view at the Sherman Adams Observation Center.

This toy-like engine powers the Mt. Washington Cog Railway.

Be warned, however, that when Mount Washington disappears into the clouds, so do you. Sometimes, though, the cog railroad climbs through the clouds to a wondrously clear top. When you return to US 302, turn right for an easy, country-perfect ride before leaving the White Mountain National Forest three and a half miles later.

In the Area

All phone numbers are within area code 603.

Eagle Mountain Resort, Jackson: 383-9111

Heritage New Hampshire, Glen: 383-9776

Mount Washington Cog Railway, Bretton Woods: 846-5404, ext. 6, or 800-922-8825, ext. 6

Mount Washington Hotel, Bretton Woods: 278-1000

Storyland, Glen: 383-4293

Index

Index

Index

Titles in the Country Roads series:

All books are $9.95 at bookstores.
Or order directly from the publisher (add $3.00 shipping and handling for direct orders):

Country Roads Press
P.O. Box 286
Castine, Maine 04421
Toll-free phone number: **800-729-9179**